Vintage Lighting

Vintage Lighting

A Collector's Guide

Barty Phillips

First published in Great Britain in 2012 by
Remember When
an imprint of
Pen & Sword Books Ltd
47 Church Street
Barnsley
South Yorkshire
S70 2AS

ISBN 978 1 84468 101 3

A CIP catalogue record for this book is
available from the British Library.

Typeset in 11pt Minion by Mac Style, Beverley, East Yorkshire
Printed and bound by Replika Press Pvt. Ltd.

Pen & Sword Books Ltd incorporates the imprints of Pen & Sword Aviation,
Pen & Sword Family History, Pen & Sword Maritime, Pen & Sword Military,
Pen & Sword Discovery, Wharncliffe Local History, Wharncliffe True Crime,
Wharncliffe Transport, Pen & Sword Select, Pen & Sword Military Classics, Leo Cooper,
The Praetorian Press, Remember When, Seaforth Publishing and Frontline Publishing.

For a complete list of Pen & Sword titles please contact
PEN & SWORD BOOKS LIMITED
47 Church Street, Barnsley, South Yorkshire, S70 2AS, England
E-mail: enquiries@pen-and-sword.co.uk
Website: www.pen-and-sword.co.uk

Contents

Contents

Acknowledgements

I am very grateful to all the people who offered advice, information and pictures for this book and especially to John and Dorothy Knight, Judith Downie, Pearson Phillips, Philippa Watkins, Jane Priestman, Joanna and Brooke Calverley, Chris Sugg, Louise Verber, Paul of Paul's Emporium, Richard of Country Oak Antiques, Lisa Beatty of Vintage Lighting, Marion of Hillwood Farm Antiques, Jayne Morris of Morris Interiors, Ron Gibson of 19th Century Lighting Co., Jeff Howard of Howard's Antique Lighting, Julia from Classic Modern, Jesse Carrington from Trainspotters, Wendy from the Antique Lighting Company, Will Hanness of The Old Cinema, Tim Bowen, Ron Taus of Leslie Antiques, Thomas Power of Genuine Antique Lighting, Isaac Pineus and Andrew Duncanson of Modernity, Susan Frost of Antique Chandeliers, Janet Holdstock of Turn On, Uli Beck of the Museum of Pressure Lamps and to Fiona Shoop for much invaluable advice.

I have also found the following websites helpful and informative:

http://dspt.perso.sfr.fr; http://marysgasbook.blogspot.com; www.abc.net.au; www.bham.de; www.about.com:inventors; www.arcadianlighting.com; www.brotheridgechandeliers.co.uk; www.buildingconservation.com; www.chandelierparts.com; www.cloudglass.com; www.colemancareers.com; www.collectics.com; www.collectorsweekly.com; www.craftsmanoutdoorlighting.com; www.cranberryglass.co.uk; www.designboom.com; www.designer-lights.com; www.enchantedlearning.com; www.essortment.com; www.fairy-lamp.com; www.heavenly-lights.com; www.howstuffworks.com; www.lampsbytiffany.com; www.lighting-equipment.com; www.madeinbirmingham.org; www.myantiquemall.com; www.nationalgasmuseum.org.uk; www.oldandsold.com; www.oldcopper.org; www.phoenixant.com; www.senses-artnouveau.com; www.stardust.com; www.biggarmuseumtrust.co.uk; www.thehistoryof.net; www.theiet.org; www.tiffanylampsandlights.co.uk; www.tinyesveld.com; www.tvlamps.net; www.wikipedia.org; www.willliamsugghistory.co.uk; www.worldaa.com

CHAPTER ONE

Early History

EARLY LAMPS

It is difficult to imagine what life was like before the days of flicking a switch to turn on the light. Sight is one of our most precious senses but one that early people could employ usefully only during the daylight hours, so during most of human history people have had to get up with the dawn to make the most of every daylight moment and go to bed when the sun went down. In the beginning firelight would have been the only way you could see at night. It also fulfilled other functions such as keeping people warm and dry and keeping wild animals at bay. Falling asleep while on fire watch or failing to find enough sticks and fuel could lead to disaster. In fact, right up to the beginning of the twentieth century, fire was still the main source of light for much of the world's population. Flaming sticks snatched from the fire could act as torches either carried around or planted in the ground. Resinous wood from pine trees was particularly good for this as the resin would flare up to give a satisfactory light, at least for a short time.

Hemlock stems, reed mace and cow parsley have all been used as torches. In substantial manor houses, a large central fire primarily for cooking also lit up the great hall. Down long corridors and into courtyards, torches on iron spikes or cressetts (iron baskets) burning oil or pitch would add brightness to a basically gloomy interior.

No wonder people have gone to extraordinary lengths to achieve even the most dismal illumination to light up the dark. For the English in the Middle Ages, the availability of good sources of lighting determined how much people strayed from home in the evening and how safe they felt returning home.

By the 1600s there were still only three ways of lighting a room: candles, primitive oil lamps or rushlights. Oil lamps remained like their forebears, shallow vessels of metal or stone containing oil in which floated a wick. They could be suspended by stout wire which might be hooked onto a convenient hook or nail. They didn't give a good light and were rarely used in grander settings such as the drawing room.

Holders for candles took several forms. There was the simple candlestick which could be placed on a table or candlestand. Paintings of this time show ordinary households with just one candle in a room often placed on a central table. In the bedroom, too, one candlestick with one candle was considered enough. The commonest candlesticks

Flaming sticks snatched from the fire could act as torches. Resinous wood was particularly good as the resin flared up to give a brightish light.

A tall, floor-standing Scottish candle-holder with hooks up the stem which enable the height to be adjusted. Its heavy base keeps it stable when at its tallest. (Photo: Country Oak Antiques)

were made of brass or bronze for the better-off or wrought iron or tin for cottagers (along with 'kitchen quality' brass by the late eighteenth century). In wood-rich areas, candlesticks and rushlight-holders were often made of local wood such as oak, pine or fruitwood.

By the nineteenth century the Lunar Society, a group of enlightened men in the north of England who met once a month to discuss things scientific, used to choose a night when the moon was full so they could see their way home afterwards. Even by the early twentieth century candles were still the main form of lighting for every day, used by students to study by and carried up the draughty stairs to bed at night and it wasn't until the beginning of the twentieth century that street lamps made it possible in many cities to walk around out of doors at night without a lantern.

This search for light has produced a wealth of fascinating lamps; wonderful and beautiful collectible objects, not just for their aesthetic qualities but for their history as well.

Timeline of lighting discoveries

Earliest times: Firelight; flaming sticks and torches

70,000 BC: Primitive lighting using hollow stones or shells

7,000 BC: Early Greek pottery lamps used with a cloth wick and reduced fat as fuel

Roman era: Oil lamps; candles

Seventeenth century: Rushlights; candles, tallow lamps

Early eighteenth century: Whale oil lamps and improved efficiency in candles; central burner invented

1780: The Swiss chemist Aimé Argand invented the central draught burner, which had a hollow circular wick

1784: Argand added a glass chimney to his central draught burner, assuring even combustion and producing more reliable light than oil lamps

1853: First paraffin/kerosene lamp introduced in Germany

1879: Edison improved a design by Thomas Woodward to produce the first successful incandescent electric light bulb

End of nineteenth century: Electric light beginning to replace gas; households still using candles, rushlights and oil lamps

Late twentieth century: Electricity supreme in lighting in the industrial world; candles only used for special occasions or power cuts and blackouts.

Darkness as the mother of invention

Anything that will burn will give some sort of light and burning branches were better than nothing, but people soon began to look for ways of creating light in its own right. Written records indicate that lamps with liquid fuel sources were used before candles of either tallow or wax. The first lights were primitive in the extreme. How desperate must those people have been who lit a wick stuck down the carcass of an oily bird such as a stormy petrel (as they did in the Scottish isles), or that of a fatty fish (as recorded in North America), the oil from the carcass itself producing the fuel? Otherwise, lights were simply hollow stones or shells filled with moss as the wick and animal fat or tallow

A slipper-shaped lamp of the type used by early civilisations. It has a flat shallow bowl for oil or tallow and a 'toe' for the wick.

as the fuel. All these primitive lamps must have given out a meagre light and lasted for a very short time, as well as being smoky with a strong acrid smell. Since those times humans have resorted to all sorts of fuels and an incredible variety of methods for providing light and there has been a constant search for an affordable solution that would provide an efficient, bright light, without the smoke and the smells.

Early lamps across the world

A fascinating amount of invention has been directed towards lamp design over the centuries. In open-air caves, lamps from the Upper Palaeolithic era survive in France, Spain, the Czech Republic and Germany. The earliest, found in the Grotte de la Mouthe in the Dordogne, France, are largely undecorated; only a few have carved handles, perhaps an indication of ritual use. In the third millennium BC, the Mesopotamian lamp, a simple slipper-shaped holder, burned sesame seed oil with a wool or reed wick. Wonderful decorative lights have been found in the royal tombs of the ancient city of Ur, in Mesopotamia. How strange that they should be placed where no eye would see them. Tomb lights were crafted in precious metals such as gold and silver and also in copper and alabaster. Off the California coast, the Catalina Island Indians quarried soapstone and carved it into lamps.

Ancient Chinese lamps were open saucers of bronze or limestone, sometimes standing on feet, with a floating wick. (The use of petroleum oil as fuel reached China in the Middle Ages, when homeowners soaked straw in gasoline and burned the mass in lamps.) Throughout the Pacific, lamps were made of coconuts also with a floating wick. Brazilians used peanut oil for fuel. In Egypt the fuel bowl had a long lip and a carrying handle. In Venezuela, nestlings of a nocturnal bird called guácharo (oilbird) were boiled down for lamp oil, and in Japan sea urchins were filled with fish oil. In many herding countries sheep skulls were used as lamps.

The Irish valued cod, seals, sharks and whales for liver oil, a smelly source of lamp fuel. Along the west coast, they salted the livers and sun-dried them to extract the oil, which they bottled and corked. To light kitchen chores, they placed lamps on the fireplace hob or fitted scallop shells in wall boxes to hold burning lamp fuel. When moving about the house, they dipped peeled rushes into liver oil and carried them held high.

Greek and Roman lamps

In ancient Greek households terracotta lamps filled with olive oil and fitted with a floating wool or reed wick were the standard for home lighting. They were often improved with a curved rim to reduce splashing. Roman lamps were similar to Greek ones but sesame oil was often used and the wick was made of verbascum or papyrus. Many were designed in bird or animal forms. In Roman Britain, householders relied on candles and oil lamps with oakum and flax wicks, which burned vegetable oil. For general purposes, the user could mount the lamp on a tall stand to spread light over a slightly larger area. The Romans are supposed to have invented the candle, and both tallow and beeswax were used.

The Roman architect Vitruvius in the first century BC described the effects of such lamps on the decorations of the home, pointing out that oil lamps blackened wall hangings, statuary and cornices. In return for the parsimonious amount of light they shed, they required continual tending by slaves, who were kept busy filling the lamps, trimming wicks, and removing the oily soot.

Pliny the Elder, the Roman commander, naturalist and gatherer of information in his *Natural History* mentions oil as a light source. In Roman settlements at Antioch, the wealthy could afford to light evening banquets with hanging lights called polycandelons which were circular brass or iron frames supporting several cone-shaped oil holders. Early Roman lamps were often sumptuous, made in carved relief, designed in the form of gods and goddesses, gladiators and mythological subjects. Such lamps might feature the god Silenius with an owl sitting on his head between two vast horns, each of which supported a lamp; or they might consist of flower stalks growing out of a circular plinth with snail shells hanging from them by small chains. All these were lit by a wick emerging from the lamp base holding a fuel such as oil or tallow. Luxurious though these lamps were, made for the powerful and wealthy, they would have produced a comparatively feeble light to our modern eyes – not much more, in fact, than the simple pottery lamps with which ordinary Roman citizens lit up their twilight hours.

In Roman Britain households relied on candles which have been used ever since in conjunction with every form of lighting. This brass candlestick is from the USA. (Photo: www.antiquesathillwoodfarms.com)

These candlesticks are all from eighteenth-century Britain, although the rushlight may be a Victorian copy of an earlier one. In the panelling behind can be seen two black marks from past candle flames burning the wood. (Photo: Country Oak Antiques)

Lamps used by the North American settlers

By the time the first settlers arrived in America nothing much had changed as far as lighting was concerned. They still would have had only the most basic implements needed for light: the tinderbox, candlestick and lantern. The grease lamp, rushlight, candle-fir (splints made from pine trees) and candle were the four types of light most often used by early Americans after 1725 for home lighting. As well as the more than 100 herbs brought over by the pilgrims in the *Mayflower* from England in 1620 to preserve their health and cure their ills, voyagers were also advised to take plenty of cotton yarn for their lamps.

Danger of fire

Throughout the centuries, efficient light was accompanied by the constant threat of fire. The fuels used were highly flammable, often explosive and fraught with dangers. It's easy to forget how dangerous lighting by naked flame could be. Although the introduction of gas lighting in the early nineteenth century made an enormous difference to many people's lives, because it was readily available without the need to constantly clean and trim the wicks or clean up the mess caused by smoke, as was necessary with oil and tallow lamps, there was still always the danger of fire. The Great Fire of London in 1666 is likely to have been started by the overturning of a lantern. In the days when many homes were made of wood, fire burned quickly and could be devastating.

The hunt for an efficient light

Since the days of the most primitive lighting – when Newfoundland fishermen created lamps out of dogfish tails stuck into a cleft stick, American Indians used euchalons or candlefish (a type of smelt found from Oregon to Alaska) in a similar way, and Shetland Islanders used stormy petrels and other oily carcasses such as penguins by shoving wicks down their throats – there has been a continuous effort to find a way of providing immediate lighting that was efficient, clean and cheap. In the constant search for adequate light, oils have been expressed from fish (a cheap oil for those living in coastal areas), animals, grape seeds, tea, cabbages, and plenty of other things, to be used in shallow vessels, oil lamps and as candles. All were luxuries in their time, although few were really pleasant to use, efficient or cost-effective.

A terracotta oil or grease lamp with decorative markings – a natural progression from the found shells and hollow stones that had been used previously.

The most common and very primitive fuels to begin with were animal fats and grease, known as tallow. Some ingenious lamps were concocted for this pretty disgusting fuel. When burned for light, tallow smelled to high heaven and its fatty odour seeped into clothing and the very fabric of the home. Tallow gave a feeble, flickering light, conjuring up terrifying images of demons, witches, giants and monsters in the semi-darkness. This was the universal form of lighting until the early Middle Ages. Even as late as 1914, British soldiers in World War One sacrificed the precious oil from their sardine tins for the luxury of providing the most meagre of lights.

Many medieval lights were made of iron and few have survived. The early English made crude earthenware lamps with a floating wick and no spout. The simplest form of light was provided by cresset stones with several depressions and these have been found in many northern parts of the world.

Primitive oil and tallow lamps

Tallow was also used in the form of candles but primitive lamps preceded the candle as a light source. Hanging stones using tallow were used to light church porches and monastery cloisters. These were made from shells and hollow stones to begin with but later they were made for the purpose rather than 'found' objects, although the earliest fabricated lamps copied the originals and were made to look just like shells. American pioneers resorted to candles, pine knots, lard-oil lamps, or saucer lamps, dishes of cooking fat topped with a twisted rag or rush wick. With this meagre oily glow, housewives completed kitchen chores and sat down after supper to mend clothing, knit mittens or dish-cloths, and repair tarpaulins and leather harnesses.

Rushlights

For centuries the only light available for household chores was daylight, limiting the workday to the hours between dawn and dusk. Women often arranged to meet and work together for such occupations as spinning or sewing, so that they could make the most of any shared illumination. The most meagre, smelliest, and least dependable light came from standard rushlights, made from porous tules or rushes. The rushes were partly peeled and then dipped in old cooking fat and mixed with beeswax, if it could be spared, to make them firmer. They were economical and therefore widely used. A 2-ft rushlight would burn for about an hour and this meagre light was the only method of illuminating homes of the poor for centuries. Even after they had been dried in the air to reduce moisture, rushlights produced a sputtering, unsteady light. The frail quality of them greatly limited the ability to work during the short daylight hours of winter.

Rushlights were still used in Europe until the end of the nineteenth century, were revived for a short time to relieve blackouts during World War Two and in rural areas were still being used until the middle of the twentieth century. They were probably not so popular in Colonial North America and the holders that do exist there may have been imported from England. However, they were certainly used and neighbours meeting at a sewing circle could turn the rotating rushlight towards their work as they searched for a dropped needle or pieced together a patchwork quilt.

Note: rushlights are not the same as rush candles. A rush candle is a block of wax or tallow that uses a length of rush as a wick, whereas a rushlight is a strip of plant fibre impregnated with tallow or grease and held in a pincer-like holder.

Candles

Obviously beeswax was preferred over tallow as it burned better, smelled sweeter and was much cleaner than crude smoky tallow candles, but it was scarce and much more expensive than tallow. Only churches and the wealthy could afford beeswax. In Christian monasteries large apiaries were kept and the beeswax used for candle-

Making candles – did you know?

- Because tallow candles smelled so strongly of animal fats they had to be kept in secure boxes to keep the rats and mice from getting at them. Sheep or cattle tallow was preferred as pork was too smelly and runny.
- Most candles today are made of petroleum, although special ones are still made of beeswax.
- By the seventeenth century European states controlled the weight, size and cost of candles and in 1709 an English Act of Parliament banned the making of candles at home unless a licence was purchased and a tax paid.
- In the late eighteenth century as a result of the whaling industry it was discovered that spermaceti, a wax obtained from crystallising sperm whale oil, was available in large quantities. This didn't smell as strongly as tallow, and was found to be more rigid than tallow or beeswax and didn't soften when it got hot. It became popular, adding impetus to the whaling industry.
- Originally candles were made by dipping the wick again and again in melted fat or wax and so were built up in layers.
- The first use of moulds for making candles was in fifteenth-century Paris, followed in the nineteenth century by a candle-making machine.
- Right up until the twentieth century many candles were still made of tallow which was the cheapest material to use. They were smelly and produced a lot of smoke and soot.
- Moulds were often made of tin, but wood and copper were used as well.

A characterful iron candlestand from North America. The tripod legs give it much-needed stability. (Photo: www.antiquesathillwoodfarms.com)

An eighteenth-century rushlight-holder with a lit rushlight perched on an oak chair of about the same date. The rush can be swivelled in its iron jaws to change the direction of the light. (Photo: Country Oak Antiques)

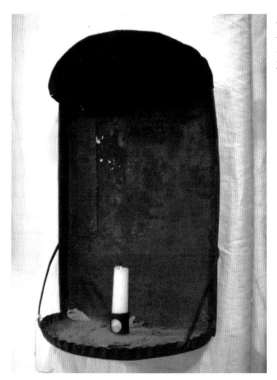

A sturdy metal candle sconce from North America with a hood to catch the smoke and help protect the flame from draughts. (Photo: www.antiquesathillwoodfarms.com)

An early nineteenth-century lantern with horn panels and a socket to slot a pole in so it could be carried around. Apertures in the lid allow smoke and heat to escape. (Photo: Country Oak Antiques)

Twisted metal pricket candlesticks like this one were used to impale the candle – pricket lamps were often used in churches but less often in domestic situations.

making. However, in England at the time of the Norman Conquest splinters of wood dipped in wax were used for lighting and the candle did not come into general use there until the fourteenth and fifteenth centuries when guilds of wax and tallow chandlers developed the industry and had control over quality. Tallow candles were made of sheep, cow or pig fat. Candles were also made of animal secretions such as spermaceti (whale oil or liquid wax obtained from the blubber of various species of whale), ambergris (a solid waxy, flammable substance found in the digestive system of and regurgitated by sperm whales) and beeswax. Colonial women in America made candles out of vegetable waxes produced from plants such as bayberries, candelilla leaves, candletree bark, esparto grass and sundry varieties of palm leaves such as carnuba and ouricury.

Candle-holders
The first primitive chandelier was the candle beam, a hanging wooden bar which held wax tapers. In churches and manor houses, candles, called wax lights, provided illumination for worship and social engagements. For domestic use, itinerant candle-dippers went from door to door creating lower-quality candles and dipped tapers from the clarified cooking fat collected by their thrifty clients.

Hurricane lamps
For lighting out of doors hurricane lamps were used. The term was originally used for any light with a glass chimney to protect the flame from being blown out by the wind. Nowadays the term usually means a practical outdoor oil-burning lamp, although it gradually became more decorative with etched glass and hand-painted chimneys. Early hurricane lamps were designed to burn olive oil, but beeswax, sesame oil, fish oil and whale oil were often used as well. They could also hold candles. Hurricane lamps helped to light homes and later, when electricity became more generally available, continued to be used on boats and trains.

Sophisticated candle-holders
Gradually utilitarian candle-holders evolved into art objects as craftsmen began to copy Holland's multibranch candelabra of brass, wrought iron, or gilded wood. High-quality candelabra came with matching candle-snuffers and shades made of horn. Gradually candlesticks developed into the more sophisticated forms of candle-holders, girandole wall brackets, looking-glass wall lights and decorative lanterns with horn panels to

shield the flame from draughts. Fragile Venetian glass provided tiers of candle-holders glittering with faceted pendants to enhance the glow. These all required constant care; the fixtures had to be lowered so they could be soaked in hot water, have the spilled wax scraped off and be given a good polish.

In sixteenth-century England, while the poor tolerated fish-oil lamps, the homes of the privileged displayed candles borne in silver sconces and brass candlesticks. Candles, too precious to be used for everyday tasks, were used to light up entertainments and special occasions. To add to the light from the fireplace, in many homes the householder might shape a piece of tin into a wall bracket or sconce with a candle-holder attached. Mirrors and reflectors helped to spread light from the source.

Candlestands of wrought iron appeared in the late 1600s, allowing the user to move the light source and raise and lower the candle as it burned down. Another room brightener was the lacemaker, or shoemaker's lamp, in which a water-filled globe intensified the light and cast shadows on walls and furnishings. Americans in colonial times often adjusted their candle-holders to burn small amounts of oil rather than candles. And when gas was introduced during the nineteenth century, many fixtures were hung on a wall like candle sconces.

Spout lamps

The spout lamp was an extension of the hollow stone. The top was enclosed and the wick inserted into a long spout rather like a teapot. Some had a double spout. The practical Dutch thought to add sand to the vessel so it wouldn't tip over. The crusie spout lamp was used from the 1600s to the 1700s by the Celts in Scotland. In the Channel Islands similar lamps were called crosset or crasset, the Cornish called them chills, but in Cornwall they also used mussel shells. Crusie lamps were also used in Europe. They had a metal bowl to hold fuel with indentations or channels to hold the wick. A similar lamp was introduced to America by early settlers in 1620 as the Betty or Phoebe lamp. The Betty lamp is thought to have been named after the German 'besser' or better, when introduced by German settlers in Pennsylvania. It could be placed on the floor or suspended from the ceiling on a hook and burned fish oil as fuel. Some had the sophistication of a double bowl to catch the drips and some could be tilted to catch the last drip of precious oil. It was still widely used in the nineteenth century, although mostly by poor households.

This interesting and elegant brass crusie-type lamp has a long, slender stem, a feature often found in whale-oil lamps. (Photo: Tim Bowen Antiques)

An early Betty lamp from North America. These lamps are similar to the Scottish crusies and Cornish chills. (Photo: www.antiquesathillwoodfarms.com)

Fuels

Whale oil

In the nineteenth century the unfortunate sperm whale was found to have a cavity in its head which contained a huge amount of spermaceti, used for cosmetics, but also a good fuel for lighting. Whale-oil lamps, often called sparking lamps, were usually small and in attractive designs with a sculpted look. They were said to be used for romantic trysts – when the oil ran out the gentleman had to leave – and also for children's night-lights. An important improvement was made around 1740 when Benjamin Franklin saw that if two tubes of a double burner whale-oil lamp were placed with a small space between them they would produce twice as much light. This discovery made it possible to make taller whale-oil lamps and became an important sort of lamp in the home. Whale oil was used as an important light source for 150 years from about 1690 to 1840. The oil was plentiful and relatively cheap.

While the whaling industry flourished, comfortable middle-class families in late Regency England and the Americas relied on whale-oil lamps, formed of a tin, pewter or brass base topped with a globe that enhanced the light, channelled smoke and heat upward, and protected against fires. These lights had numerous shortcomings: sperm oil was tricky to light and required a short wick to heat the viscid oil, which tended to thicken quickly as it cooled.

Lard

When whale-oil prices rose, lard became a popular alternative fuel. Lard lamps were widely used in the 1830s to 1850s. They were of unique design – the burner heated up and liquefied the lard, so the reservoir was only as large as necessary for the burner to reach the fuel. Many designs were patented and a good number of lamps marketed. All followed the basic idea of a heat-conducting material (usually copper) going down into the lard. The wick was usually flat, though some were curved round the conductor and they often had several wicks. Lard lamps were often made of tin, though occasionally they might be glass or pewter. The canting fount or English student lamp was a version designed to tilt so that the wick could be kept immersed in the oil.

Colza oil

A popular lamp oil during the early nineteenth century was colza oil, made from rapeseed, cabbage, kale and the roots of swedes. It burned well in lamps, providing the link between the early teapot-shaped lamps and the much more efficient paraffin lamps of the mid-nineteenth century. Most colza-oil lamps had a reservoir often shaped like a classical urn to one side, which in some fittings obstructed the light. The reservoir presented a problem for single lamps, casting a shadow over much of the room. In later variations this problem was overcome by introducing a pump to carry the oil up to the wick in the Moderator lamp, and in the Sinumbra lamp which appeared in the 1820s, the reservoir was designed as a hollow ring inside the rim of the shade above which reduced the shadow.

Camphene

After the 1850s, whale oil and lard were both overtaken by the highly volatile mixture of turpentine and alcohol known as camphene, a dangerous explosive causing several disastrous fires and the loss of many lives. Also known as Porter's fluid or burning fluid, gasogene and camphorated gas, camphene was introduced in 1837 and large quantities of alcohol were employed in making this mixture until the introduction of petroleum for lighting. The fluid was burned in a lamp provided with a wick and the lamp was lit by igniting a little alcohol placed in a cap surrounding the wick. In spite of being highly explosive, it became popular and largely displaced whale oil. Camphene lamps were distinguished by

Early paraffin lamp and burner without a chimney; this single-wick burner has a handle, so would have been intended to be carried from room to room.

the long tapering wick tubes with thimble-like caps to prevent the camphene from evaporating when the lamp was not in use.

Paraffin/kerosene

Candle and oil lamps continued to be the main light source for homes until the end of the nineteenth century. Lamp oil, known as paraffin in Britain or kerosene in the USA is a refined form of petroleum or of coal and bituminous shale. The refining or distilling process was discovered in Germany in 1830 and the first paraffin lamps came from there. However, paraffin was improved and patented by a Scotsman, James Young, in 1850. He founded a company known as Young's Paraffin Oil Company, and paraffin eventually ousted all other similar fuels in the 1850s. By 1848 paraffin was being produced from mineral oil in England. Six years later the first factory for the manufacture of 'coal oil' was established in the United States.

The oil wells discovered in Pennsylvania produced around 400 gallons a day and the refining of this new fuel helped to produce the sophisticated oil lamp with a reservoir in the base. Paraffin/kerosene lamps produced a good bright light in a more convenient way than previous lamps and remained popular until electric light became widespread. But they were not without their inconveniences and certainly their dangers.

The Argand lamp

Around 1780 Aimé Argand, a Swiss physicist, experimenting with a gravity-feed tubular wick with a spreader or air diffuser fitted into the central burner created the central draught burner. A few years later, finding that the current of air through the inner tube was failing to give the brilliance to the circular flame that he was looking for, he placed a metal chimney over the flame and immediately had a clear steady light. Later his partner, Quinquet, significantly improved this design by introducing a glass chimney instead of the clumsy metal one.

A large peasant-style cottage in rural Eastern Europe has a hanging paraffin lamp and not much more in the way of lighting other than what comes through the windows.

The Argand wick light thus consisted of a substantial reservoir, a tubular wick, and a glass chimney with a bulge shading steady, smoke-free illumination which enhanced the amount of oxygen feeding the flame. The glass chimney prevented the flame from being blown out and was narrow in one place to create the right amount of draught. The lower part of the cotton wick soaked up fuel in the tank and capillary action transferred it to the burner. Argand's lamp assured even combustion of lard, fish oil, vegetable oil, and mineral oils (paraffin/kerosene). The Argand burner had the great advantage that it was designed to fit any lamp fount. For the poor, the lard or fish-oil Argand lamp, manufactured and patented in England by Matthew Boulton of Birmingham in 1784, was an excellent answer to ordinary household needs.

In 1782 with the introduction of the Argand burner, home lighting improved dramatically. When Argand and Boulton lost their patent two years later, several other manufacturers quickly stepped in with affordable innovations as well as new styles and fuels for the wealthy and upper middle-class which rapidly changed the possibilities of lighting the home. There were simple, functional designs such as wall lights with the reservoir designed to reflect the light downwards to light a work surface or dining table and there were many elegant but functional brass reading lamps. More sophisticated versions might have the reservoir in the form of a classical urn at the centre of a table lamp with one or more lamps bracketed off it.

One disadvantage of the Argand oil lamp and its many imitators in the early 1800s was that the best oil then available, colza (made from the turnip family) was so thick and viscous that it had to be fed to the wick either by gravity from a reservoir above or pumped up from below. In 1798 B.G. Carcel invented a portable clockwork-driven lamp to help force the oil into the burner. A Parisian, Franchot, patented the Moderator lamp in 1836 which had a circular wick and a piston driven by a spring to force fuel upwards.

An eighteenth- or nineteenth-century English paraffin/kerosene lamp with a reflector to help direct the light.

Different types of paraffin/kerosene lamps

There were three main types of paraffin lamp: wick lamps, mantle lamps and pressure lamps. Between 1859 and 1870 around eighty patents a year were applied for concerning oil lamps, the research being aimed at producing better light. Draught design of the burner and the chimney together as a unit was the key factor.

This brass paraffin/kerosene lamp has a single wick which can be clearly seen through the glass chimney.

Many lamps were designed specifically as pendants, like this slim oil lamp with its large smoke-catcher, seen hanging in a window.

The duplex burner

In 1865 Joseph Hinks invented the duplex burner which used two flat wicks side by side and an extinguishing device. The duplex burner was reliable and efficient (and is still used today practically unchanged in greenhouse heaters and lamps). In detail designs differed; some had a wick adjustment mechanism, for example.

Different types of wick lamps included barn lamps or lanterns, tubular lamps invented in the late 1860s which circulated a mixture of fresh warm air back to the flame through side tubes, improving the burning efficiency, but all wick lamps were smelly if the oil or paraffin/kerosene was of poor quality or the wicks were not kept clean or the adjustments were not correct.

The Kosmos lamp

The Kosmos lamp, made in Germany by Wild & Wessel, took a flat wick which became circular in the burner. The draught was still taken from the sides of the burner as in the flat-wick type and the burner had no spreader. The Kosmos burner was confined in use to small hand lamps and reading lamps. The central draught burner had a tubular wick and a hollow draught tube in the centre which produced a more efficient flame and most had a flame spreader in the centre of the tubular wick. The wick went up through a tube which provided the correct mixture of air to the burner and when ignited produced a clear bright yellow flame.

Wick lamps without chimneys

Glass chimneys and globes were fragile and difficult to pack up for export to the ever-widening market of foreign countries and colonial frontier posts, so a number of designs produced lamps driven by a clockwork fan to provide a natural draught and a clear flame without a chimney at all. The Wanzer, the Britannic and the Hitchcock were among the first in 1868. The Kranzow was made in Birmingham by Sherwoods, quantities of which were exported all over the world. They continued to be produced until the middle of the twentieth century.

Mantle lamps

The mantle or incandescent lamp was an important variation of the wick lamp. In 1828 a Swedish chemist Johan Berzelius managed to separate the oxide of thorium from one of the element's salts, though he had no idea how it would eventually be used. In 1835 the Englishman William Fox Talbot found that blotting paper impregnated with calcium chloride left a white ash with a peculiar bright afterglow when burned. These were the first tentative steps towards the brightly burning mantle lamp, although the first real mantle was not realised for another fifty years. The difference in design was that the burner was set below a conical mantle made of thorium or other earth material that incandesces when heated in a flame. It gave a much brighter light and often needed a lampshade. It was greedier in fuel and produced a lot of heat which meant it didn't smell as strongly as other forms of lamp and the sooty deposits could burn off, making it cleaner. Because they burned at a higher heat, mantle lamps were sometimes used to heat small buildings in cold weather. One disadvantage was that if the lamp was adjusted wrongly, it could cause flames to come out of the top of the chimney, sooting up the mantle and releasing a large amount of soot into the room.

Pressure lamps

The pressure lamp, often known as the Tilley lamp in Britain and the Coleman lamp in the United States (after their manufacturers in those countries) was a sophisticated design compared with wick lamps and produced a brighter light although it could be complicated to use. There were many types but basically the principle was simple: the pre-heating with methylated spirits of a generator tube. This sort of lamp had a fuel tank at the bottom with a small pump to pressurise the paraffin. It had a narrow flue at the top of the lamp and above that, a burner. The mantle was a fabric bag coated with chemicals which glow brightly when heated by the flame.

To work a pressure lamp the paraffin had to be heated to vaporising point because vaporised paraffin burns hotter than the liquid fuel, so the paraffin was heated with a

primer, usually methylated spirit, burned in a small tray underneath the burner. The paraffin in the tank was then forced into the burner by pumping up the air pressure in the fuel tank, forcing the paraffin up through the flue. When the burner was primed to sufficient heat to vaporise the paraffin, the pressurised paraffin was forced into the hot burner where it was vaporised. This vapour was directed down into the mantle where it was hot enough to make the mantle glow and produced a bright white light.

This early student lamp with its reservoir on one side and the light source on the other would have been used much as it is seen here, on a desk.

Oil lamps to the rescue

In Britain most chimneys and globes were imported from France, Belgium and Germany, and when German supplies dried up in 1914 because of World War One, quantities were made in Britain, although of inferior quality. By World War Two oil lamps had largely become outdated but when electricity supplies were interrupted by bombing, oil lamps were brought back into use when necessary. The main problem was finding glass chimneys that would work efficiently. Home-produced glass chimneys had to be used but the most critical factor of an oil lamp is the draught supply, which is calculated accurately. The chimney is all-important and requires the size and location of the bulge and the overall height to be precisely correct. Luckily stocks were found in warehouses and oil lamps provided essential light for homes.

The introduction of gas lighting

The first gas used for domestic lighting in the West was made from distilling wood and coal and was first introduced towards the end of the eighteenth century. At that time many people still viewed gas lighting with suspicion. Although by 1816 26 miles of gas mains had been laid in London for factory and street lighting, few homes adopted it before the second half of the nineteenth century. Despite the introduction of the many improved forms of lighting, candles remained the principal source of light in most houses throughout the nineteenth century and continued to be popular for special occasions, even in houses where gas lighting had been installed. Lighting with oil or gas cost around twice as much as tallow candles, so for the less well-off homes, and for everyday use, candles still played an important role.

Distillation of gas

Gas has been produced by distillation from all sorts of materials including coal, wood, whale oil, even walnuts. Development of gas for lighting was part of an international scientific research and contributions came from many countries including Britain, European countries and America. In Britain, attempts to manufacture gas from coal appear to have begun in the late seventeenth century. The reason why gas for lighting was first developed to a usable standard in England may have been to do with the political situation in Europe, where progress was difficult because of unstable governments. Philippe Lebon, for example,

This gas street lamp with its ornamental lantern shade shows the gas flame clearly.

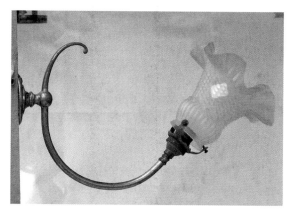

This frilly French lampshade on its curved brass bracket is typical of the designs of domestic gas lamps when they were first introduced.

who patented his 'thermolampe' using gas distilled from wood in 1799, was murdered in the prime of his life in revolutionary Paris. Most of the European experimenters used wood as their raw material for gas. In England, however, where coal was widely available, that became the raw material of choice and, curiously, when British capitalists set up gas industries in countries where wood was readily available, they still chose a technology based on coal.

The first house to be lit by gas

William Murdoch (or Murdock), a Scottish engineer living in Cornwall, began experimenting with gas derived from coal in 1792. His house in Redruth was the first to be lit by gas but he never patented his invention and made no money from it. The German inventor Friedrich Winzer, who changed his name to Winsor when he came to England, was the first person to patent coal gas light in 1804. David Melville, an American of Scottish ancestry, received the first United States gas light patent in 1810 and the first US home to be lit by gas was that of William Henry, a coppersmith in Philadelphia.

Gas from a central works

Winsor, a keen and successful entrepreneur, was the first person to consider supplying gas from a central works rather than from individual installations and he was also the founder of the first public gas supply company in the world, the Gas Light and Coke Company in London in 1807. From then on large towns and cities rapidly set up their own gasworks. Among the economic impacts of gas lighting was that it meant much longer working hours not only at home, but in factories. Factories, public buildings and streets were the first to be lit by gas because existing oil lamps and candles provided sufficient light for the life that existed in most homes and practically all homes had an open fire. The new street lighting actually provided extra light to upstairs bedrooms in many town houses, so that once you'd found your way to the bedroom you could put the candle out to get into bed.

Following the discovery of petroleum in Ontario in 1857 and the drilling of the first commercial oil well in Titusville, Pennsylvania, fossil fuels began to supplant animal

Early lighting accessories

Lamps burning fuels required several accessories so that they could be lit, kept clean and put out when necessary. The various containers used to hold the fuel or the candles were as varied as necessity and imagination could provide. The list of early accessories needed for lighting was enormous:

- Spills and splints for carrying a flame from the fireplace to the lamp: people had to rely on these for lighting their lamps. Spills are paper thinly-rolled and splints are shards of wood; both could be lit from the fireplace and carried to the lamp. Eventually holders for these items were created, sometimes designed to co-ordinate with the lamp itself.
- Sulphur matches in the form of little sticks of pinewood with sulphur on their ends may have been used in ancient Rome, but the safety match was not introduced until the 1850s. They were used to transfer the fire from the tinder to light a spill. The tinder was then extinguished by smothering.
- Tinderboxes were probably a very early invention. They evolved from boxes of dug-out wood to sheet iron, brass, and leather. There were even pocket tinderboxes that could be carried around when away from home. They were essential to keep the strikers, flints and sulphur matches handy and tinder of shavings dry.
- Tinder pistols or 'strike-a-lights': a generation of lighters which were mechanical tinder-lighting devices. The early 1800s saw complicated contraptions that used dangerous chemicals such as hydrochloric acid, zinc and hydrogen or sulphuric acid, potassium chlorate, sugar and gum arabic.
- John Walker's friction lights: in the US these made tinderboxes obsolete. They were the predecessors of today's matches. When pulled quickly from between a folded sheet of glass paper, the tip, coated with a gummed mixture of chlorate and antimony sulphide ignited into flame.

An interesting collection of early nineteenth-century lighting equipment including in the foreground a tinderbox with candle-holder built into the lid. The metal striker and flint are lying in front and the fabric (lit to sustain the flame while the candle was lit) peeps out of the box. (Photo: Country Oak Antiques)

Wick-trimmers were important to keep the lamp from smoking or failing to burn well. (Photo: Country Oak Antiques)

- 'Rushnips', 'boxes' or 'balconies' were the names given to the holders of prepared rushlights waiting to replenish those that were used up.
- Snuffers: these were shaped like a pair of scissors with a box on top to collect the carbon residue on top of the wick. Carbon residue was called snuff, hence snuffers. They were also used to extinguish or 'snuff out' the flame. The point on the snuffers was used to straighten the wick before trimming it. Early sixteenth-century snuffers were made of iron. Brass, bronze and polished steel were used from the early- to mid-eighteenth century. The design of the snuff box varied over the years. The first was heart-shaped; the next was a semi-circle evolving to a fence blade and variations of the rectangular box. Both boxes and handles were decorated. They were often in cast-iron but might be brass with silver-plating. A later improvement was the addition of a spring which kept the blades in alignment and ensured that the glowing snuff would be safely kept inside the box once it was trimmed.
- Wick-trimmers: a wick becomes uneven when burned, so trimmers were used to cut a straight line to encourage the lamp to burn more efficiently.
- Dousing cones: these were cone-shaped and used to extinguish burning candles.
- Candle boxes: every home would have some kind of candle box to make sure there would be candles ready when the ones in use burned down, either on a table or hung on a wall. They were made of wood, brass, sheet iron or tin.

Purely decorative:

- Prisms: probably introduced during the seventeenth century, prisms were cut glass shapes that would hang round the collar of a light catching and diffusing the light in their many different facets; not so much accessories as part of the design of a lamp.

and vegetable oils. Gaslight was economical, and householders liked the clean, bright, odourless combustion, which enabled cooks, for example, to continue working on winter afternoons when natural light faded early.

The incandescent mantle

The amount of light which could be produced by a wick was limited by the surface area of the wick and the amount of fuel and air able to reach it, as fuel burns at the top of the wick only. The gas mantle, on the other hand, provided a much larger three-dimensional surface and was far more effective as a result. Invented by Carl Auer von Wesbach in 1885, the incandescent mantle was the last major breakthrough in oil and gas lighting of the period, before both gave way to electric lighting. The mantle consisted of a skirt of silk or cotton impregnated with a non-inflammable mixture suspended over a fierce flame. When first ignited, the cotton burned away leaving fine, brittle filaments of non-combustible material in its place which glowed white hot or 'incandescent'. The mantle worked best with either gas or the fine mist of paraffin produced by a pressurised reservoir, producing a bright, warm light to rival an electrical bulb. This type of pressure lamp is still widely used in camping lamps today. Von Wesbach was granted a master patent for his incandescent mantle in 1885. The mantle was made of a fine ceramic gauze fibre impregnated with chemicals from rare earths and when heated by a Bunsen flame glowed to a white incandescence that was much brighter than the reddish-yellow light that came from flat flame burners. By 1891 the company was claiming that the mantle gave up to 60 candle power for 3,000 hours. These improvements brought the price down, produced better light and helped to stave off competition from electricity, at least for the time being. Nevertheless, early gas mantles were not very efficient and were fragile. When a home-owner bought a gas fitting he might find the mantle already broken by the time he got it home. Gas in the home also meant installing ventilation grilles in the cornices and ceilings.

Private gasworks

Wealthy homes had so many oil lamps that lighting had become a small domestic industry in its own right with special 'lamp rooms' dedicated to cleaning and filling the oil reservoirs and staff trained to do this. At first gas was despised, considered a rather demeaning form of lighting, suitable for the masses and beneath the dignity of better-off homes. It was not until later in the century that gas lighting became fashionable inside wealthy homes. Often such homes were based in the country and the urban supply was not available to them so they had to build their own private gasworks in their own grounds. From the 1860s many well-off families were making good use of the luxury that brighter lighting afforded and many had a variety of hanging gas lamp pendants, wall brackets and mobile table lamps, illuminating different parts of the home.

Gasworks for the gentry

In 1857 George Bower of St Neots in Huntingdonshire patented a portable gas-works especially for 'mansions, villas, manufactories, and railway stations'. The smallest would provide gas for six to eight burners for four hours, each giving a light equal to ten ordinary candles. Larger portable gas 'works' could burn up to 500 lights. One of his selling points at the time was that:

> The object of this invention is to place within the reach of all who require an apparatus extremely simple, subject to little wear and tear, and so arranged as to be readily managed by any ordinary labourer or domestic servant.

Its advantages, according to his advertisements, were:

1. It occupies but little space; an apparatus for 6 to 8 lights requiring not more than from 60 to 80 sq ft
2. It is simple in construction, requires but little labour to manage, and the fire may be lighted and permitted to go out with the same impunity as an ordinary shop or hall stove
3. A retort, when worn out, can be replaced by a new one without the assistance of a skilled mechanic
4. It is adapted for the production of gas from wood, peat, oil or any description of coal
5. There are no fire-bricks required for setting the retort other than those which are sent with the apparatus.

Although gas lighting transformed nineteenth-century life, early gas lamps provided only a modest yellow light and were smelly. Other disadvantages were that it was hot and made the atmosphere in the room stuffy by taking oxygen from the air. All gas appliances produce heat. In houses lit entirely by gas, especially when they used open flame burners, a third of the heating of the house came from the gas lights. This could be convenient, cleaner and economic but the temperature varied enormously through the house and would have created a lot of draughts. The answer in large homes and public buildings was to connect the lamp to the outside air by providing a chimney. This formed a passage for the heat from combustion and the whole fixture became a means of ventilation. Such lamps were known as ventilating lamps. As lighting fixtures were always high up on the wall, where the temperature was hottest, these ventilators

A North American gas wall fixture still with its gas tap and decorative detailing; it has a typically charming etched glass shade. (Photo: Howard's Antique Lighting)

worked efficiently. They were often attractive, well-designed and made to conform to the particular decoration of the room or building.

Suspended gas lights were known as gasoliers. They had a counterweight and slide mechanism, allowing the height of the light to be adjusted and servants could raise and lower them for easy cleaning. The sliding mechanism was filled with water to provide a seal and fitted with fishtail or Union Jet burners. Globes and shades mimicked the shapes of those on Regency-era oil lamps, but the new gas lights required no bulky fuel reservoirs. These predated the gas mantles that appeared in the later 1880s.

A problem for all lighting technologies was that light shone upwards. Attempts had been made to invert the gas flame but these were not popular for use in the home. When an inverted burner more suitable for domestic use was invented in the final years of the century, it was immediately successful. This inverted burner offered all the advantages of electric lighting at a fraction of the cost and moreover it was possible to convert upright gas fittings through the use of an adaptor.

Gas burners

Gas released from any natural source will catch fire easily. Natural gas from rotting vegetation can produce spontaneous 'fire wells'. These have always been a phenomenon and the early Chinese are said to have collected gas from natural fire wells into animal bladders and, by piercing holes to let the gas escape, to have created

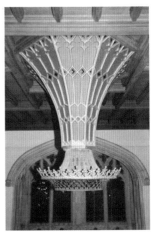

This splendid ventilator was built by William Sugg and installed in a building in Surrey. The large brass pipes and apparatus for carrying away the heat and gases were hidden away in cupboards within the walls of the building. (Photo: Chris Sugg)

This Auerbach mantle burner, produced by William Sugg, could be used upright or upside-down. The white incandescence produced a bright steady light. (Photo: Chris Sugg)

torches. The first gas manufactured from coal was simply burned through a hole or series of holes in a pipe, known as an open flame burner. The introduction of burners consisting of iron caps pierced with one or several holes improved efficiency but they corroded quickly and luminosity varied greatly. These burners were often named after the shape of the flame they produced, e.g. rat tail, cockspur, batwing, fishtail, dovetail.

Fluctuating quality

The quality of the lighting depended largely on a variety of considerations: the quality of the coal, the pressure of the gas from the gasworks and the care the consumer took in cleaning and changing their burners regularly. In 1851 Samuel Clegg of the Gas Light and Coke Company introduced gas Argand burners that had a ring of small holes to be used with glass chimneys. The burner produced a ring of bright light but the flame smoked if it wasn't continually adjusted when the gas pressure fluctuated. Legislation in England was enacted from 1851 to produce gas to a specified illumination and purity that were subject to regular inspections and testing and William Sugg, a notable English manufacturer of the time, introduced a non-corrodible burner tip in 1858, called the Christiana, which reduced these problems of poor quality light considerably. Sugg had the foresight to send many of his employees to design college to ensure that every product was designed professionally. The two types of improved open-flame burner with which he was involved were the Christiana and Argand interior fixtures. Another design produced by David Sugg, William's son, was the Cromartie, offering an entirely different form of open-flame gas lighting. Sugg also introduced simpler open-flame designs such as the tee bar pendant and later the swivel wall brackets that pull out from the wall to bring the simple single open-flame light source closer to the user. Von Auerbach's incandescent mantle eventually superseded all other gas burners in light output and economy and helped to keep off competition from the electric lamp for many years.

This is a similar burner used to produce a light directed downwards with a clear glass shade with slightly frilled edges. (Photo: Chris Sugg)

The first street lighting

Gas lighting was used at first mainly for street lighting. In June 1807 Pall Mall became the first street in Britain to be lit by gas. In the United States Baltimore was the first city to light its streets with gas in 1816. By the early nineteenth century some of the streets in most cities in Europe and the United States were lit by gas. Originally gas was only used for lighting for a few hours at the start and end of each day. It was soon realised that it would be more efficient to produce larger quantities at a time and store it, so the first gasometers were built. The first gas holders consisted simply of a 'bell' floating in a tank of water. Calibration marks on the floating bell showed how much gas was being made and how much was being used.

Gas on the wane

The development of electric lighting at the turn of the nineteenth century in Britain and the USA threatened to replace gas lighting in homes, but gas continued to be popular in households for lighting and it was not until after World War One that builders began to install electric lighting systems in all new homes. In the 1930s gas lighting for streets gave way to low pressure sodium and high pressure mercury electric lighting.

Gas museums

A few former gasworks still exist as museums of the gas industry. They provide a fascinating story, often with artefacts and information from the time. They include the National Gas Museum in Leicester, England, which contains many fascinating displays in a Grade II listed gatehouse of the former Leicester Corporation Gas Works built in 1878, and the Biggar Museum in Scotland. The Norwegian Petroleum Museum in Stavanger opened in 1999 and has exhibits on all aspects of oil and gas; the Drake Well Museum in Titusville, Pennsylvania tells the story of the beginning of modern oil industry with videos and exhibits.

Electricity – lighting at the flick of a switch

Arc lamps

Even while gas lamps were still being developed, scientists were experimenting with electric light. When Sir Humphry Davy (1778–1829) observed the dazzling effect of the arc created when two pieces of carbon a short distance apart are connected to a high voltage electricity supply, he inspired the search for practical, affordable and efficient lighting by electricity. Arc lamps are too harsh for indoor home use but their discovery and early use is important in the history of electric light. During the next seventy years several engineers used the arc to make practical electric lamps. However, the batteries were too expensive to provide an affordable source of light. By the 1870s cheaper batteries and practical generators were becoming available

Milk glass globes were always popular for electric lighting since they helped to diffuse what was considered to be uncomfortably bright light. This is an industrial shade from Eastern Europe from the early 1900s. (Photo: Trainspotters)

and engineers turned once more to electric lighting. The first arc lamp to be used in large numbers was the Jablochkoff Candle developed in 1876 by a Russian telegraph engineer. Throughout the 1880s and 1890s arc lamp installations became common and London's Victoria Embankment became the first street to be permanently lit by electricity. Arc lamps were always far too bright and harsh for use in the home and after 1910 there was little further growth in this type of electric lighting because more efficient types of filament lamp were developed. The arc lamp did, however, launch the careers of many notable electrical engineers and proved to the public that electric light was a practical reality.

How a filament bulb works

In an incandescent filament light bulb the heated wire or filament was first made of carbon and heated until white hot (incandescent) by passing an electric current through it. When electricity is applied it is converted to heat in the filament. The filament's temperature rises until it gets rid of heat at the same rate that heat is generated in the filament. The filament reaches a high temperature, generally over 2,000 degrees Celsius. In a standard 75- or 100-watt bulb the filament temperature is roughly 2,550 degrees Celsius. At high temperatures like this, the thermal radiation from the filament includes a significant amount of visible light. Early experiments show that it was not a simple procedure because it needed a filament material that could withstand being heated to white-hot temperatures and then cooled without breaking. Researchers had to find a way of sealing the connections in a glass bulb without the heat cracking it and of creating a vacuum pump to remove enough air to prevent oxidation. Experiments with metal filaments showed that they could run at a higher temperature than carbon. Platinum was used in early tests but was far too expensive for mass production. Metals with high melting points were tried and eventually tungsten was found to have a higher melting point than any other metal.

Development of the light bulb

One of the first pioneers of incandescent electric light bulbs was Heinrich Goebel, who around 1854 had the idea of lighting his clock and watch shop in New York by electricity and set about creating a light bulb with a carbon filament. This German-born American had noticed that carbonised bamboo fibres could become incandescent in a vacuum. He is said to have used bottles of eau de cologne to make his first light bulbs and his own bamboo walking stick to make the filament. However that might be, Goebel was way ahead of his time and failed to get any interest from manufacturers. He was not alone in trying to produce an incandescent bulb; many others were researching the same thing and among them was Thomas Edison who, seeing a display of arc lights, realised that they were far too bright for domestic use and decided that the light had to be 'diluted'. He turned his attention to the incandescent filament bulb, 'the less promising line of enquiry'. Unlike all other experimenters at the time, he envisaged from the start not just the bulb, but a whole lighting system which could compete with gas lighting.

This is a modern filament light bulb of the kind most often used in Britain, with a bayonet fitting.

During the late 1800s Edison in America and the English physicist Sir Joseph Swan in England were each working separately on the idea of the incandescent light bulb. Swan showed his model to a meeting of the Newcastle Chemical Society in 1878 but couldn't actually demonstrate it working because he had burned out the filament in a lab test! He did give a well received demonstration in 1879 but by that time Edison was well advanced in his version. Swan formed a public company but in October Edison kept a lamp burning for thirteen hours and patented his bulb. Edison's first bulb sold for $2.50 each and he opened his first electric light factory in 1880, closely followed by Swan in England who opened his outside Newcastle in 1881.

A pretty little Tiffany-style lamp using stained glass for both shade and stem, made for electricity.

Swan successfully sued Edison over infringement of his British patent. Eventually they came to a business agreement and formed the Edison Swan Electric Light Company (Ediswan) for manufacture and marketing of light bulbs in Britain. Today Edison's screw bulbs and Swan's bayonet fittings are still manufactured and sold.

At the Paris International Electrical Exhibition in 1881 and the Crystal Palace Electrical Exhibition in 1882, Edison's and Swan's light bulbs were shown alongside those made by other inventors.

Timeline for the development of the electric light bulb

1809: The first ever electric light was invented by Humphry Davy, an English scientist. He experimented with electricity and invented an electric battery. When he connected wires to the battery and a piece of carbon, the carbon glowed, producing light. Other scientists began experimenting with electricity to produce light too.

1850: Edward Shepard invented an electrical incandescent arc lamp using a charcoal filament. Swan started working with carbonised paper filaments the same year.

1854: Heinrich Goebel, a watchmaker, produced a light bulb which had a carbonised bamboo filament placed inside a glass bulb and was claimed to last up to 400 hours.

1860: Swan began trying to make carbon-based incandescent lamps that would be practical and long-lasting. These worked but had a short life because the vacuum was poor.

1875: Henry Woodward and Matthew Evans patented a light bulb.

1878: Swan's lamps became more successful after better vacuum pumps became available. He used a carbon fibre filament derived from cotton.

1879: Thomas Edison created the first truly successful incandescent light bulb in America. He discovered that a carbon filament in an oxygen-free bulb glowed but did not burn up for forty or so hours.

1880: Swan patented his own version in an incandescent bulb lighted by a nitro-cellulose carbon thread; Edison continued to improve his light bulb until he produced one that could glow for over 1,200 hours using a bamboo-derived filament. Since then the incandescent lamp has been improved by using tantalum and later tungsten filaments which evaporate more slowly than carbon.

1882: Lewis Latimer, a member of Edison's research team (known as Edison's Pioneers), developed and patented a method of manufacturing carbon filaments.

1883: Establishment of Ediswan, the Edison and Swan United Electric Company.

1903: Willis Whitney invented a metal-coated carbon filament that would not blacken the inside of the bulb (a predecessor of the tungsten filament).

1906: The General Electric Company was the first to patent a method of making tungsten filaments for use in incandescent light bulbs. The filaments were expensive.

1910: William David Coolidge invented a tungsten filament which lasted even longer than the older filaments. The incandescent bulb revolutionised the world and is used for most lighting to this day.

1920s: The first frosted light bulbs were introduced; neon lighting introduced.

1950s: The halogen light bulb was introduced.

1960s and 70s: Better reflectors and mirrors for even brighter bulbs.

1980s: Low-wattage metal halides introduced.

1990s: 60,000-hour magnetic induction light bulb invented by Philips; popularisation of new environmentally friendly bulbs.

The first electricity station in New York City

In the United States the first electricity station, built in New York City on Pearl Street in September 1882, provided service to one small neighbourhood, enabling home-owners to illuminate their residences with flame-free, clean, odourless and controllable lighting. By 1900 Sears, Roebuck was advertising a wide range of domestic lamps. There were desk lamps, kitchen fixtures, and light sources for the dining room. Rapid development of the home lighting market resulted in such innovations as the rheostat light dimmer, a feature of Frank Lloyd Wright's Robie House, built in Chicago in 1908. The following year, General Electric began producing Osram bulbs, a German invention employing tungsten filaments. These economical bulbs used at least 50 per cent less electricity than bulbs with carbon filaments.

In America Edison and his research team designed all the components and accessories required for a complete electrical installation, such as parallel circuits, fuses, switches and meters. Swan in Britain did not do the same and these products were developed piecemeal in Britain, and in the early years it was left to those responsible for installations to design the systems and make the components resulting in installations that were not always safe or satisfactory and could sometimes be quite bizarre.

Slow start for electric lighting

Initially gas lighting was slow to give way to electricity in both Britain and America partly because to begin with electricity was so much more expensive than gas, and the ordinary person could not afford it. It was not until about 1911 when metal filament bulbs had been much improved that electric lighting became more widely available. Even by the end of World War One electric lighting was still only enjoyed by the wealthy minority. It was only when the Electricity (Supply) Act of 1926 was passed in Britain that real progress was made in distribution. However, by the 1920s, homes lit by electricity had become common in towns and cities in all industrialised nations. Yet even in the 1930s, poor people living in the country, far from power plants, had still to rely on oil lamps, candles and lanterns for their lighting.

Lord Armstrong at Cragside

Despite this slow start electric lighting, when it did arrive, soon became popular, although for many years it was limited to people living in urban areas. Some of the wealthier households couldn't wait and had the lights installed before there was an electricity station to make them usable. The only option for anyone living outside the reaches of the local supply station was to have their own generating system installed. The costs of electrical installation, lamps, fittings and accessories could be enormous, so it was only the wealthiest who could afford it. Cragside, the country retreat of Lord Armstrong, built on a bare and rugged hillside above Rothbury became one of the most modern and technologically advanced houses for its time in Britain. In the 1880s, the house had hot and cold running water, central heating, fire alarms, telephones, a Turkish bath suite and a passenger lift. Most remarkable of all, it was

Antique light bulbs

- At first the electric light bulb had enormous novelty value and the earliest fittings displayed the bulb quite prominently.
- Perhaps the most surprising thing is how many different light bulbs have been invented and manufactured in the search for efficient and affordable light. Early bulbs were available in a wide variety of shapes and patterns, often highly ornamented, but as the novelty value wore off and the short life span of the bulb was recognised, attention turned back to the shade and the fittings themselves.
- With the introduction of metal filaments in light bulbs around 1906, there was a huge demand for bulbs and many glass-blowers were employed to make them. The process was not automated until around 1920.
- As collectibles light bulbs are classified as 'early technology'. They may seem a peculiar interest, but they are considered important in industrial development as artificial lighting was what created a much longer working day. They can also be considered curious, interesting and often aesthetically pleasing.
- Collectors may specialise in collecting the different bases, the different filaments, the different bulbs produced by particular manufacturers or the various figural bulbs which may be flame, candle-shaped or in the shapes of flowers, animals and other things.
- Bulb design and filaments varied enormously. Early carbon filaments were made of carbonised cardboard, bristol board and cotton string. There was carbonised bamboo and asphalted carbonised bamboo, the GEM filament (high temperature carbonised cellulose) and osmium and titanium filaments. There were round bulbs, globular bulbs, narrow bulbs; in fact a seemingly infinite variety of bulbs.

A Victorian-style room boasts electric lamps with fabric shades and many-branched candelabra still sitting on the mantelpiece.

the first house in the world to be lit by hydro-electricity. A collection of early carbon and metal filament bulbs can be seen in the Visitor Centre at Cragside, now owned by the National Trust.

Many people were tempted to cut costs in a variety of ways. You could have a number of lamps on one circuit but if one lamp failed, all the lamps on that circuit would fail (like some Christmas tree lights) and as the bulbs were sensitive to fluctuations in current, this would happen fairly often. You could also lay the wires not within the wall but running along them (which was marginally safer, giving the poor insulation of early wiring). Many private households chose to have low-voltage installations and some had generating sets and accumulators that were inadequate with maximum load.

In the late 1950s, engineers at General Electric, still pioneers in lighting technology,

A modern bedroom uses old paraffin/kerosene lamps converted to electricity as stylish bedside lamps. Their height gives a good light when reading in bed.

invented the tungsten halogen lamp. This used a high temperature tungsten filament inside a special halogen-filled quartz envelope. The combination of the halogen gas and the tungsten filament produced a chemical reaction known as a halogen cycle that increased the lifetime of the bulb and prevented its darkening by redepositing tungsten from the inside of the bulb back onto the filament. It produced a strong, bright white light with an efficiency about 10–15 per cent better and generally a much longer life than ordinary incandescent lamps. Their compact size and high colour temperature made them extremely popular in display spotlighting and 'high tech' luminaires for which they are still used today.

Early in the twentieth century as electricity became cheaper and more widespread, electric lighting became a selling point in new homes. Often it was installed in formal rooms but not every room. At this stage, no specific style had been found for electric lighting. Fittings were unimaginatively either made to look like candles or to look like the gas fittings that had gone before them. In fact, until 1900 many manufacturers simply sold their gasoliers as electroliers rather than develop designs more suitable for electricity.

Cheaper light bulbs

When the Edison & Swan master patent expired in September 1893 their bulb prices were slashed and bulbs became cheap to buy. From then on the company faced fierce competition from other manufacturers, particularly those who obtained licences to manufacture a new generation of bulbs that were being developed abroad. Bulbs with metal filaments began to appear in the late 1890s but by the time the initial difficulties had been ironed out, they were almost immediately superseded by bulbs with tungsten filaments, first introduced in 1909 and by 1914 bulbs were not only more efficient but much cheaper as well. However, the lights often flickered and dimmed progressively as the load on the batteries increased.

Because a perfect vacuum could not be achieved in carbon bulbs, the filament gradually deposited carbon particles on the inside of the bulb which caused it to blacken. Although consumers were advised to change their bulbs when this began to happen, it was expensive to replace the bulbs and many people continued to burn their dim lamps until the filament broke completely.

Some light on light bulbs – did you know?

Over the years, the tungsten filament light bulb has been far and away the most popular for the home.

- American Peter Cooper Hewitt patented the mercury vapour lamp in 1901. This was a high-pressure arc lamp that used mercury vapour enclosed in a glass bulb. Mercury vapour lamps were the forerunners of the fluorescent lamp. Mercury lamps were coated with phosphors and ultraviolet radiation making them fluoresce and providing light. The colour depended on the type of phosphor chosen.

- In 1927 Friederich Meyer, Hans Spanner and Edmund Germer patented a low-pressure arc lamp, the fluorescent tube. They were introduced to the general public at the New York World Fair in 1939. Fluorescent tubes give about four times as much light per electricity consumed as incandescent bulbs and last longer. They became popular as working lights and for chain stores because of their shadowless quality and the good colour reproduction they achieve. Fluorescent light was found to be four times more efficient than incandescent with a bulb life of ten to twenty times as long. However, to begin with the light was found to be harsh and unfriendly and in the main fluorescent tubes tended to be used for work environments and in the home for workshops and kitchens.

This is a filament bulb made by hand with an Edison screw fitting – similar to the early light bulbs. The sharp point at the bottom is part of the hand-making procedure.

- Now compact fluorescent tubes are made in many sizes and configurations and can be used in the place of incandescent bulbs, colours are better and they are cheaper and longer-lasting. Compact fluorescent lamps (CFLs) have a rather cold light, even the so-called 'warm' colours are workmanlike rather than comfortable. They also have a more diffuse light and cannot offer that sparkle to glass and metallic objects offered by tungsten filament bulbs. Since the 1970s tungsten halogen lamps have become popular in the home, especially in kitchens and modern interiors where their bright, sharp lighting complements the clean lines and metallic finishes.

- In 1959 a patent was granted to Elmer Fridrich and Emmett Wiley for a tungsten halogen lamp, an improved type of incandescent lamp and in 1960 a General Electric engineer Fredrick Moby took out a patent for his tungsten halogen A-lamp that could fit into a standard light bulb socket.

- Recent advances have continued to focus developments on greater energy efficiency, longer life and lower environmental impact. Towards the end of the twentieth century, the compact fluorescent 'energy saving' light bulb became more and more accepted, both for domestic and commercial applications. One innovation, the compact fluorescent lamp, burned brighter than traditional bulbs without producing more heat, required less electricity, and outlasted other bulbs. It was considerably more expensive, however. Because of growing concerns about the costs of energy, along with anxiety over supply and possible shortages, this type of product seemed likely to light kitchens of the future.
- During the late 1970s the low-voltage bulb was introduced which operates on a supply of 6, 12, or 24 volts rather than a mains supply of 240 volts in the UK and 100 volts in the USA. Most low-voltage bulbs are much smaller than conventional bulbs and almost any fitting can be made in a low-voltage version. Low-voltage bulbs are economical to run, sometimes producing two or three times more light for the equivalent wattage in standard light bulbs. They generate less heat and have a life of 2,000 or more hours.
- In line with this trend, lighting based upon light emitting diodes (LEDs) is now starting to emerge. These have excellent energy efficiency and extremely long operating life, but have yet to achieve the brilliance or colour-rendering properties of other technologies.

CHAPTER TWO

Periods and Styles

You might not expect fashions in lighting to change much when the only forms of illumination were candles or tallow dishes. Nevertheless, adequate lighting was something to be proud of and candle-holders of all kinds were things that the good housewife would want to show off, so candle-holder designs did change over the centuries.

The quality of candles improved with the introduction of steatite (a sort of soapstone), the discovery of whale oil and later with paraffin wax (which is the main component of modern candles). As more candles were introduced into better-off homes, two or three candles might be lit at the same time in the main room and there would be different types of candlestick for different situations. At first lights were seldom, if ever, left burning in rooms with nobody in them; they were more likely to be carried from room to room to bring light to dark areas. Candlesticks designed to be carried like this had handles and sometimes a protective shade to prevent them blowing out.

The beginnings of a brighter future

Although fashions in candle-holders of all kinds did change over time and during the seventeenth century the very rich were able to afford the latest in inordinately expensive rock crystal chandeliers, in the main until the middle of the nineteenth century changes in lamp designs were in the detail rather than in the concept and were often to do with greater efficiency and practicality rather than aesthetic style. The moment paraffin/kerosene lamps became available, lighting design began to take off. As lighting became more sophisticated and more efficient and available forms of fuel became the norm, any designer worth his salt wanted to design lamps. The story of lighting from the eighteenth century onwards becomes ever more varied and decorative.

Lighting for the needs of the home

By the middle of the nineteenth century light was considered not simply a luxury but a necessity in the home as elsewhere. Even in poor homes there would be several lamps, to read by, to work by, particularly in the kitchen and to see you up to bed. In large, wealthy houses, there might be as many as forty lamps, providing full-time occupation for one of the servants who was put in charge of ordering and storing the fuel, keeping the wicks trimmed and replaced, the reservoirs topped up, the glass washed and the brass clean and polished.

In the drawing room there would be lamps for general background light and for reading, probably duplex lamps or central draught lamps. These might be table lamps with ceramic bases or standard lamps with brass pedestals. They could be highly ornamental, chosen to fit in with the furnishings of the 'best' room.

There were specially designed reading lamps for the study or library and special lamps for the billiard room; one type consisted of a suspended ceiling fitting with arms for four independent oil lamps with cut glass reservoirs and green shades carefully angled to throw the light downwards onto the table and not to glare into the players' eyes. Hanging or pendant lamps suspended by chains from the ceiling often had smoke-catchers to try to prevent the ceiling from becoming blackened by the soot from the lamp. In the kitchen there would be rather more utilitarian lamps, either pendants and/or several wall sconces. But candles were still used in every home as a supplement to oil lamps and were often still the way people would light their way to bed.

Some popular decorating/lighting styles

Lamps have taken on a bewildering array of shapes, forms and techniques and this is an indication of the main historical styles of particular periods. All dates are flexible; styles too, were flexible and varied from country to country as follows:

1700–1810 Federal: this United States style has gone through many revivals and is based on the founding fathers' architecture including many early public buildings, Colonial-style homes and plantations. The original lighting consisted of real candle fixtures, candle chandeliers, candelabra, candle lanterns, various candle hurricane lamps and candlesticks and towards 1800, oil lamps and whale oil lamps. Many of the fixtures were made of tin or iron, sometimes combined with wood and looked primitive, while others were crafted in pewter, brass and silver and looked comparatively elegant. Lighting found today in this style is likely to be reproduction.

This interior has an eighteenth-century feeling with its furniture lined up against the wall and an elegant mirrored wall sconce to reflect the light from the candles.

1714–1837 Georgian: Georgian style covers over a century under the reigns of the three British Georges and is sometimes divided into the Palladian, early and late periods. It is characterised by elegance, harmony, symmetry, pale colours, delicate furniture and lighting designs. Paraffin/kerosene arrived during the Georgian period, so look for chandeliers with curved octopus-like arms, swan-neck wall sconces and elegant silver candlesticks.

1643–1715 Louis XIV: baroque style with weighty brocades of red and gold, thickly gilded plaster mouldings, glitter, and magnificent chandeliers reflected in enormous mirrors.

1715–44 Louis XV: magnificent French styles including rococo and chinoiserie.

1744–93 Louis XVI: French classical revival.

1840–1901 Victorian: the Victorian age lasted for a long period and at a time when England's power was expanding. Fashions and styles changed many times, influenced by new discoveries of different parts of the world and harking back to previous ages. Electric light didn't reach the Victorians until after 1880. Up until then homes used elaborate candelabra and chandeliers and many oil lamps. By the middle of the century, there were elaborate gas-powered sconces and gasoliers. So there is no one Victorian style, and French rather than English influence was equally strong on American and European lighting design including the beginnings of Art Nouveau.

1900–40 Neo-classical: dominant in domestic design in the USA; classical symmetry, classical ornaments, pillars and pediments.

Rococo style very much reflected the glittering and unreal life of the French court. Here a rococo candlestick stands in front of an ornate French woven tapestry.

1910–29 Spanish Revival: late 1800s' European-trained architects designed hugely stylish houses for the wealthy. Lighting of this period was made of wrought iron and sported stylised leaves and berries.

1920s–30s Art Deco: the roots of Art Deco grew out of Art Nouveau. It was the first movement to see lighting as an integral component of the house, rather than as individual light sources and used a mixture of decorative styles, mainly characteristics from various avant garde painting styles of the early twentieth century.

1920s–30s Modern Movement: the Modern Movement rejected all forms of unnecessary decoration and coined the phrase 'form follows function'. Its leading practitioners were Walter Gropius, Mies van der Rohe and Frank Lloyd Wright, the Bauhaus School and Russian Constructionalists. The lighting consisted of perfectly

Lighting styles up to 1900

- 1840–60 Rococo Revival: also known as French Antique, Rococo was an architectural and decorative style of early eighteenth-century France, characterised by generous, detailed shell and foliage carvings, often becoming asymmetrical. Rococo Revival lamps were originally powered by gas and were highly intricate with asymmetrical scrolls, crosses and lavish carvings of cornucopias, fruits, birds, flowers and foliage. Look for grapes, acorns, lots of leaves, shells with cranberry, engraved or frosted and cut glass shades.
- Late 1700s–late 1800s Gothic revival or Victorian Gothic: a series of gothic revivals which began in mid eighteenth-century England and spread through the nineteenth century to Europe. Characterised by gas lighting and sconces with use of medieval motifs such as trefoils, quatrefoils, crochets, pinnacles, cluster columns, pointed arches, all inspired by the Middle Ages and church and cathedral architecture.
- 1860–80 Second Empire: named for the reign of Napoleon III (1852–70) who undertook major building campaigns to transform Paris into a city of grand boulevards and monumental buildings; the style used decorative brackets and lots of crystal, echoed in castles and palaces all over Europe.
- 1875–85 Eastlake Period: in the United States this style was developed after the English architect Charles Eastlake who wrote a book economically called *Hints on Household Taste in Furniture Upholstery and Other Details* in 1868 which became influential in America; similar to Arts and Crafts style. Lighting included paraffin/kerosene lamps and gas lighting. Ceiling and wall fixtures were made of iron, spelter, 'pot metal' or brass. Most were simple in design, rectilinear, often of flat construction; no curves.
- 1875–85 Aesthetic movement: examples from Greek, Japanese, Persian, Moorish, Egyptian and other exotic styles. Also motifs from nature and two-dimensional patterns, natural forms simplified and stylised.
- 1890–1900 Turn of the century: all antique lighting styles were used in combination with gas and electricity introduced within a short period; soon gas became obsolete and electricity became the primary light source.
- 1894–1914 Art Nouveau: French/Belgian name for an art movement taken up in Europe and the United States, inspired by nature and lithe young women's bodies.
- 1895–1910 Arts and Crafts (in America also called 'Craftsman' or 'Mission' style): rebellion against mass production – artists were employed to make pieces individually by hand. A reaction against the clutter and variety of earlier Victorian

styles. Simplicity and use of natural materials were paramount. There was plenty of woodwork, mostly oak. Light fixtures were made for gas/electric combinations and electric use, mostly in brass or iron. Stained glass table lamps were made with square oak frames and square oak bases. The decoration of fittings came close to Art Nouveau as they had graceful flowing lines and lack of a specific historical influence. The rise of the Arts and Crafts movement coincided with the emergence of electric lighting and although many new homes in Britain continued to be built with gas lighting until World War One, many of the leading Arts and Crafts designers such as W.A.S. Benson were associated with electric light fittings.

A no-nonsense North American Mission-style chandelier on a square four-arm frame is combined with simple pink glass shades. Such chandeliers were popular in the late nineteenth century.

formed white glass globes of different shapes on simple hanging or flush-mounted bells, casting an almost shadowless light. Metal was also used for many lamps.

1940s–80s Designer lighting: inventive designs and new styles making use of modern lighting technology and materials spearheaded in particular by Italian and Scandinavian designers.

Fashions in candle lighting

Candles, rushlights and primitive oil lamps were still the only forms of lighting during the seventeenth century although in 1749 an oil lamp *Àrévebère* was invented in Paris with a reflector to increase the light. Candle lanterns were used in corridors, halls, stairwells and other draughty places so the candle wouldn't blow out. They were usually made of metal with glass windows. Later lanterns became more elegant and could be seen in smart surroundings, hanging over dining tables, together with candles on the wall. Single candlesticks were used throughout the house; some were made with handles so they could be carried from room to room. Often during the early 1700s they were made with square bases and might have the family crest as the only decoration.

The single candlestick

There are two basic types of candlestick: the pricket type and the socket type. The pricket is simply a spike and the candle is impaled on it. Pricket types were made of wrought iron, cast brass and bronze and were used a great deal in churches. Socket

These two candlesticks are made of carved wood and would have made a handsome pair on a sideboard or dresser. (Photo: Tim Bowen)

candlesticks became much more popular in the home and an enormous number of socket candlestick designs evolved through the centuries. Design details (drip-pans, bases, shapes etc.) changed from decade to decade. Since in the 1600s and 1700s homes were still almost entirely lit by candles, ordinary everyday candlesticks were simple, made of wood, brass or pewter, with a handle if they were intended to be carried from room to room. Paintings of ordinary households of the time often depict a bedroom or living room with just one brass candlestick and one candle, which was obviously considered sufficient.

Georgian candlesticks were often taller than previous ones, giving a wider spread of light. Candlesticks for the main rooms were often highly ornate and made of carved giltwood, of ormolu (gilded brass) and porcelain with gilding, or ormolu and bronze *patiné*, sometimes painted. Silver was popular and so was silvered bronze and if they were very special they could be of rock crystal and *vermeil* (another term for silver-gilt). Around the 1730s an added sophistication was devised consisting of a 'pusher-ejector' in which a button or nut was screwed or riveted to the end of a rod on the underside of the base. This was used to push the candle gradually upwards as it burned down and finally to eject it.

From 1720–70 rococo style began to evolve in France and its spiralling, spinning designs were taken up all over Europe. The light-hearted intimate themes of rococo suited interior design and were popular for light fittings. They were whimsical, ornate and elegant, featuring shells, palm leaves, dragons and flowers.

Candelabra and girandoles

Portable, free-standing multiple branched lights with nozzles arranged in a circle were known as girandoles or candelabra. They were popular used on candlestands and on tables or sideboards. They could be in the form of bouquets and classical figures such as Cupid and Psyche or Zephyrus and Flora were popular. The 'stick'

Only the greatest houses could boast a carved and gilded candlestand as gorgeous as this with so many candle-holders to light up a splendid salon. The candles have been gilded to match the décor.

was often in the shape of a Corinthian capital. The designs for these were often inventive and not just in the shape: in some the arms could be unscrewed to reveal pot pourri containers (probably a practical idea since candles could be very smelly). Some had built-in adjustable shades to help in diffusing and directing the light.

Candelabra were for special occasions. They were expensive, and often made of silver especially for the dining table or sideboard. The less well-off would buy them in Sheffield plate at a third of the cost of silver. They sometimes stood on plinths or *torchères*, one in each corner of the drawing room. The lights were mostly placed close to the walls to give a flickering illumination that would highlight the mouldings and strange rococo decorations in the room, often elaborately carved themselves and causing macabre shadows.

A sumptuous great hall has an enormously tall multi-branched candlestand in the centre and more in the corners to give as much light as possible to welcome guests.

Candlestands

A candlestand was a tall upright table, often on a tripod, designed to hold a candlestick so that the light was raised up high and enabled wider illumination. Candlestands were still unusual in England in the 1640s but by the 1650s elaborate stands were being made in Paris. When the English got around to having candlestands in elegant rooms, they favoured tall ones, in spite of the risk of them toppling over and causing fires. The French, if they wanted a support for a branched candlestick and there was no console table to stand it on, introduced sturdy pedestals or *guéridons* which were more practical and certainly safer. Candlestands could be placed anywhere in a room, but it was safer and more usual to put them against a wall. In 1706 at a masked ball in Paris four young noblemen dressed up in gold with golden masks and silver sashes like carved gilt *guéridons*, wearing candelabra on their heads, and stationed themselves in the four corners of the room.

Candle shades and screens

Candlestick lamps: candles could be converted to slightly more aesthetic candle lamps by attaching metal, silk, parchment, card or paper shades to them. These protected the candle from draughts so that it gave a

Splendid ballrooms in the time of Louis XIV and Louis XV were often panelled with elaborate mirrors which would reflect the crystal chandeliers and candle sconces to create a magical atmosphere.

The triad

Around the seventeenth century candles began to be used in connection with mirrors. A much-adopted feature for elegant rooms from the lighting point of view was the 'triad', a suite of table, looking-glass and pair of candlesticks designed to go together as a group with the looking-glass on the table and the candlesticks standing on candlestands at either side of it. This became a popular ornamental feature from the 1670s until the early eighteenth century. They were often set up between two windows. However, the candlestands with candelabra sitting on top of them used to get in the way of the curtains and must have been a dangerous fire hazard, which is perhaps why the pull-up curtain evolved during the last twenty years of the century. The candlestands were a nuisance, liable to get knocked over and went out of fashion by the end of the century as a component of the triad and the candelabra were placed on the table instead of next to it – much more sensible. Even when they were removed from the triad they were still used in other parts of the room, especially in the corners.

---

steady light without flickering or blowing out. The problem with these candle lamps was that, as the candle burned, the shade had to be constantly adjusted to keep the same comparative height as the candle or it would catch fire. Several devices were developed that would keep the candle at the same height while it burned and also would support the shade. One was Green's Patent Arctic Lamp for Candles patented by a Mr Green of Hatton Garden in London, in which the candle was enclosed in a metal tube and forced up by a metal spring as it burned. The idea was that it would fit most candlesticks and was made to look like an ordinary candlestick. Polalite lamps, patented by a different manufacturer, were of almost identical design.

Curious though it may seem to our modern light-saturated eyes, when there was no other light in the room, candles could seem dazzling, so small screens that clipped onto the candlesticks were often used in libraries or studies where people might want to read or write. There was also a style of branched candlestick which had a lampshade just like those used today, known as a *garde-vue* and made of paper or metal. Scholars studying by candlelight often used such a screen attached to the candle, not only to protect their eyes from the glare of the flickering flame but also so as not to diminish the precious light on the pages of their work. Such screens were called candleshields and were commonly made of a reflective material to make most use of the available light. The first candleshields were patented in 1817.

Student candle lamps

A type of lamp specifically designed for studying and reading appeared in the eighteenth century and became so popular that it remained in use until the end of the nineteenth century. It consisted of a metal candle lamp with a hooded metal reflector which concentrated the light on the books being read. The candle was spring-loaded in a metal tube (like Green's Arctic Lamp and the Polalite) so that it remained at the same height even as the wax melted. By 1913 this lamp was so successful that a version in nickel plate called the Holborn Candle Reading Lamp could be bought cheaply. Some reflector lamps had an eye screen attachment to prevent the eyes having to deal with the flickering flame, and others were telescopic so that the height could be adjusted to suit the particular situation.

Candle sconces

More sophisticated candlesticks were branched with a candle-holder or nozzle at the end of each branch. The branch could project from a table candlestick or from a plaque or sconce hanging on the wall. The words wall lamp and sconce are often used interchangeably to describe lighting attached to a wall. Strictly speaking, however, the lamp was the thing that provided the illumination, while the sconce was the piece that was physically attached to the wall usually in the form of a brass dish or plate sticking out from the wall to reflect the light. If it had repoussé decoration it was called a 'plate candlestick'. These plates were usually made of brass but cheaper ones could be of tin. The back plate might be of mirror glass which reflected the light better than polished metal.

During the eighteenth century candles began to be used with mirrored sconces and these became popular. Smart homes were beginning to include mirrored glass in their decorations and gilding and, of course, they also helped to augment the light with their warm gold colouring and glittery surfaces. Sconces and candle branches attached to mirrors became a feature above the mantelpiece where the candles would increase the light by reflection. In fact the reflections could be so effective that candle shades were often considered necessary to protect the eyes from glare, while at the same time candle reflectors enhanced the illumination.

In the late 1700s a candlestick lamp was manufactured which was adapted from a bedroom candlestick to provide a lamp which would give a steady flame, even in draughty places. It had a metal base of silver, brass or bronze and a high glass funnel which slotted into the

A highly decorative gilt rococo sconce with crystal droplets, acanthus leaves and gilding. This one has been converted to electricity.

A simple but comfortable cottage dining room with upholstered dining chairs and a pretty little mirrored sconce next to the window that will reflect and enhance the candlelight.

base. The metal body below the funnel was pierced to create an upward draught of air. Sometimes these candle lamps had glass globes instead of funnels to protect the flame. The candle was often enclosed in a spring device to keep it at the same height as it burned. This fitment was adapted to wall candle-holders for railway carriages.

Chandeliers

Hanging light fixtures with multiple candles have been used for hundreds of years. As a way of lighting a room from above with several candles, chandeliers have a long history. To begin with, there were the primitive wooden pieces holding just a few candles that probably hung in medieval grand halls. They were little more than a cross-shape formed of two pieces of wood with a spike (pricket) at each end. The candles would have been of tallow rather than wax and would have lent a dim and flickering light to the enormous dark interiors of medieval churches, abbeys and castles across Europe. Few chandeliers of this period have survived the destruction of churches and monasteries during the Reformation in the sixteenth century though similar simple chandeliers were still being made in Victorian times.

But most of us have a vision of a chandelier as a glittering waterfall of sparkling crystal drops. These works of wonder stem from the seventeenth century and some of the most wonderful were made during the time of Louis XIV. Chandeliers of beads and rock crystal mounted on wire armatures (like later lead crystal chandeliers) hung in a number of splendid French interiors before the 1670s. Charles II owned one in 1667, for which a protective case was made of 'taffeter and ribbons' for when it was not in use.

There are innumerable different styles and designs for chandeliers. This one is designed like a crown of candles which branch out from a central brass bowl, complementing the beautifully decorated plaster ceiling.

Types of chandelier

Antler chandeliers: made of the antlers of a deer, elk or sometimes moose. Large antler chandeliers are popular in hunting and mountain lodges but smaller varieties can make a grand impression in country homes.

Arts & Crafts or Mission chandeliers: these have a boxiness; often a central metal ceiling mount branches out to several short angular arms that hold squared, downward-facing milk glass lampshades. The shades are often decorated with metal detailing or stained glass segments.

Beaded and shell chandeliers: these are similar to crystal chandeliers but use beads or shells instead of crystals. The capiz shell with its mother-of-pearl finish is a favourite element in contemporary designs. A beaded or shell chandelier is much lighter in weight than a crystal chandelier and therefore not so complicated to install.

Candle chandeliers: this type of chandelier has existed since the Middle Ages in various forms made of wood or metal. Nowadays almost all candle chandeliers have been converted to electricity.

Crystal chandeliers: probably most people's idea of the classic chandelier – a romantic ideal for people looking for elegance and old-world charm, these chandeliers can be large or small, tall or short, often using cut glass dangling from the arms and sometimes hanging in swags between the mounting frame and the arms to reflect light and create a shimmering effect. Elaborate crystal fixtures on the grand scale were considered chic in Europe in the eighteenth and nineteenth centuries.

Metal chandeliers: simple designs with several streamlined arms leading to lights that may be placed under lampshades or inside glass cups. The arms are often s-shaped or otherwise curved, though modern designs favour more geometric lines. Popular finishes include brass, brushed nickel and wrought iron.

Murano glass chandeliers: originally crafted in the glass-blowing island of Murano near Venice in Italy. Much Murano glass is made of silica using a technique in which the silica becomes liquid at high temperatures. There is a moment when the glass is soft enough to be shaped just before it hardens. Murano glass can be found in many colours, the bright transparency allowing the light and colour to play off each other.

With the general increase in luxury more candles were burned so there was much greater illumination in many rooms after dark. The French developed a method of casting glass in large plates in the 1680s and glass mirrors began to be used extensively in smart interiors reflecting the numerous flickering flames from the chandeliers. These were difficult to produce and as a result inordinately costly, especially the silvering, but they enhanced the natural light and reflected candlelight prettily. Such mirrors were often used as wall panelling, an exceptionally expensive way of decorating a room at that time.

Rock crystal chandeliers

Chandeliers were not necessarily enormous fountains of glass droplets but could be of ormolu with perhaps six elegant arms holding one candle each. In the sixteenth century Venetian bronze fixtures were often encrusted with glass flowers. But most of the crystal chandeliers we are familiar with came from seventeenth-century France and early eighteenth-century England. French chandeliers were lavishly ornamented with cut and faceted rock crystal (pure quartz), which refracted the light to give a brilliant effect.

The first reflectors used in chandeliers consisted of shining brass plates and light-breaking rock crystals from the earth to spread and reflect the light. Rock crystal was difficult to get, brittle, hard to work with and expensive. Pressed glass pieces could be used as an alternative but these were dull because they lacked the qualities of refraction and the glass was also brittle and could not be cut and shaped like rock crystal. In 1676 when George Ravenscroft developed his new crystalline glass resembling rock crystal he added lead oxide to the glass during its manufacture, making the material easier to cut. It also refracted light better than rock crystal.

Chandeliers were sometimes so tall that they hung low down in a room and as wigs were also tall, there was a risk of getting your wig caught in the mechanism, with presumably, the rather nasty possibility of your hair catching fire. However, such grand chandeliers were only seen in the wealthiest of castles and palaces. Huge crystal chandeliers were uncommon except as status symbols for the rich. Even when they were permanently installed, they might well be there simply to impress rather than for practical purposes. (When George III visited Bulstrode Park in 1779 it was noticed that the chandelier in the hall was being lit in his honour for the first time in twenty years.)

This unusual little chandelier has a long 'icicle' hanging from the centre. This would be suitable for a traditional Victorian eighteenth-century hallway or a 'boudoir' or small salon.

Chandeliers in France and England

Seventeenth-century French chandeliers were lavishly ornamented with cut and faceted rock crystal which brilliantly refracted the light. The most expensive chandeliers were made of moulded or faceted glass. Rock crystal chandeliers probably reached their peak in the court of Louis XIV, the Sun King, and the style is still recognised as *Louis Quatorze*. Chandeliers might range from 4ft to 8ft in height, carry hundreds of candles and thousands of crystals. They were suspended from the ceiling with a mechanism for raising and lowering the whole structure so that it could be reached to change the candles and light them. In Paris even high society might not buy enormously expensive chandeliers as permanent fixtures but would often simply hire them for balls and receptions.

This large classical chandelier has strings of large droplets in a formal design. Even in grand mansions such chandeliers might be hired for special occasions rather than installed permanently.

By 1765 the elegant style of Robert Adam in England produced crystal chandeliers that were slimmer and longer. The design of the shafts of the chandelier were often based on Grecian urn designs; their arms were strung with chains of pendants and their candle sockets and drip-pans became very elaborate in the form of bells or flowers.

The discovery of lead crystal

George Ravenscroft developed an ultra clear glass (flint glass) in 1674 and in 1676 added lead oxide to his glass to create a more brilliant sparkling effect. The glass could be cut and polished and became known internationally as lead crystal. It was used to make beads and droplets of moulded or faceted glass for chandeliers. Lead crystal was much cheaper and easier to work than rock crystal which it completely replaced by the middle of the eighteenth century. By the end of the century small drops of glass would be strung round ormolu frames to reflect the candles around the room in glittering sparkles of glass. Throughout the eighteenth and nineteenth centuries English chandeliers were among the finest in the world and by the middle of the nineteenth century had reached enormous size and complexity. Alongside these luxurious marvels, manufacturers also created more modest chandeliers of many styles and sizes for the middle classes.

By the nineteenth century the names of individual designers and manufacturers of chandeliers began to be acknowledged. In England there were William Parker, William Perry and F. & C. Osler; there was Baccarat in France; Schonbek and Swarovski in Czechoslovakia; Lobmeyer in Austria; the Mount Washington Glass Factory (Pairpoint) in America and many more.

Crystal chandeliers – did you know?

- Georgian crystal is often recognised by its blue-grey colour. This was known as Derby Blue as the most suitable lead mined in Derbyshire produced this colour. It is now thought of as attractive but it wasn't popular in the home and created a problem for the manufacturers of the time. By 1816 most manufacturers were using purified lead oxide which eliminated the blue tint.
- Counterbalances were included in the suspension rope or chain to make it easier to light the candles.
- These chandeliers gobbled up candles and were not considered suitable for daily use because the light was thrown upwards rather than usefully down onto work or books.
- Households now began to benefit from the invention and creativity that went into designing fixtures, certainly for the great and the grand. Ceiling pendants with many branches often had thousands of glass droplets to reflect and refract the light. There were circular iron 'château' chandeliers, 'barn' chandeliers, gilded brass together with rock crystals and draped strings of glass beads hanging in festoons underneath tall chandeliers.

Murano glass chandeliers

Around 1700 pretty and curvaceous blown chandeliers began to be made on the island of Murano. By the end of the eighteenth century chains of cut glass buttons began to appear on chandeliers. They were crafted by lapidary cutters using the same styles used on jewellery and were referred to as paste; these buttons gave such bright fires of colour on their edges that by the Regency the preferred design was to have chains of descending buttons rather than large stem pieces. By the nineteenth century chandeliers could be mass-produced using steam-driven cutting wheels. Some of the examples made by F. & C. Osler in Birmingham were extraordinarily lavish and included a 27ft-high fountain for the Great Exhibition in 1851.

French and other European palaces of the seventeenth and eighteenth centuries were panelled with ornate mirrors to reflect the dozens of candle sconces and chandeliers, as this detail shows.

Revolutionary changes in lighting

The Argand lamp

The invention of the Argand lamp in the 1780s completely changed the way rooms looked after dark and also changed the way the rooms were used. Whereas before, lamps used to provide only enough light for one person to see by, the Argand lamp, with its steady flame, produced enough efficient light to enable several people to sit together for such things as sewing or reading music, so evenings took on a different pattern and a whole family could play cards or take part in other games or activities as a group. Most light, however, in less sociable rooms or poorer households was provided by individual candles.

Paraffin/kerosene lamps with coloured glass reservoirs were effective and pretty objects. The Argand burner would fit most such lamps.

From 1820 to 1870 there were important developments in lighting. The Argand principle was improved upon and paraffin/kerosene fuel was introduced in 1853 which offered much more opportunity in terms of different designs for lamps and offering a brighter light. Later on, gas lighting became commonplace which meant, of course, that you could light up various parts of the room by turning on a tap. The level of lighting increased generally, greatly heightening people's expectations and providing a challenge for designers who quickly became aware of the effects of light on different colours and textures. Gas lamps were usually provided with Victorian glass shades which gave the lamps their peculiarly pleasant and gentle quality. But one unfortunate feature of gas lighting was that although it gave more illumination more easily, it also suddenly made certain colours look sickly and drab, it was not flattering to the complexion and was said to make even diamonds look dull.

In 1893 Thomas Fell and John Ulrich designed a floor-standing or hanging angle lamp, which replaced centre draught lighting, creating no shadow as it replaced the top-mounted burner above the font with a movable burner set on a hinge. The user could lift off the bowl and refill it without extinguishing the flame.

Types of lamp to look for

Student lamps

The student lamp was a unique kind of kerosene/paraffin oil lamp with several distinct engineered features that set it apart from other forms of lighting. Early student lamps were simple and purely functional with the fuel holder on one side of the 'stem' and the lamp and shade on the other. Some might be of a very basic design with a reflector to

Student lamps were made with large, often green, shades to eliminate glare from the eyes and to cast the light downwards onto the work. This double one would give a good working light.

direct the light onto a desk. Later student lamps became much more elaborately decorated. Shades and chimneys were produced in glass of many types and colours, embossed satin and gloss opalescent or acid-etched. Manufacturers included Tiffany, Manhattan Brass, Plume & Atwood, Bradley & Hubbard, Edward Miller, Handel, Revere, Parker and Wild & Wessel.

Library lamps

Nineteenth-century kerosene/paraffin hanging lamps popular in the United States combine some of the most decorative period metalwork with fine glass shades. The styles ranged from simple cottage-style lamps to high-style nineteenth-century art glass masterpieces. Such lamps were a focal point in the library or dining room of Victorian homes. Glass shades, fonts and smoke bells could be plain or opalescent patterned in cranberry, ruby, pink, blue, amber, vaseline, Burmese, cut-velvet, cameo or mother-of-pearl, painted with floral or scenic motifs. Coloured jewels and prisms decorated the shade-holder band. They often had embossed fonts and intricate castings of flowers, cherubs, birds, starbursts and the ever popular dragonfly. The grandest were even more spectacular than parlour lamps from the same period.

Parlour lamps

These are sometimes called 'Gone with the Wind' lamps after the famous movie. Popular in the United States, they were originally oil lamps, highly decorated, lavishly hand-painted and lacquered with colourful glass globes and fonts held by ornate metal fittings. They usually had a small metal smoke bell suspended above the burner. Stem lamps had a long stem and were intended to sit on a table. Finger lamps were short and had a small handle so they could be carried about the house. They were made in all kinds of glass, including clear, opaline, cranberry, ruby, green, amber, satin, cased, and mother-of-pearl, often with lavish patterns. The Sandwich Glass Company, Atterbury, Hobbs Brockunier, Riverside, US Glass, Duncan and Fostoria all made such lamps.

Leaded lamps

These were created for kerosene/paraffin and later electricity, made with a variety of glass types with intricate castings in bronze, brass and white metals for the bases. There was an astonishing variety of leaded stained glass lamps for the turn-of-the-century home. Early kerosene/paraffin oil leaded stands were made with more translucent glass to make the most of the available candle-power produced, but electric lamps were more opaque to subdue the brightness of the light and were directed downwards.

Manufacturers included most famously Tiffany in the USA but there were a number of other US manufacturers who made Tiffany-style lamps of good quality, such as Duffner & Kimberley, Philip Handel, Quezal and Steuben. There were several other commercial imitators who manufactured leaded glass or bent-panelled shades. Such lamps can still be found throughout the US and Canada. Williamson and Co., Gorham, Wilkinson, Bigelow & Kennard, John Morgan and Sons, Suess Ornamental, Unique Art Glass and Metal, J.A. Whaley, and A. Hart are all names to look for. If you would like to see lamps made by some of these companies, the Association of Stained Glass Lamp Artists has a website showing dozens of stained glass lamps: www.leadedlamps.com

Leaded lamps, whose jewelled glass pieces glowed with wonderful colours when lit were popular. This little desk lamp would produce a friendly light on a side table or small desk.

Miniature lamps

A petite form of kerosene oil lamp was introduced during the nineteenth century. These were used as night-lights in the bedroom or as discreet lighting for romantic trysts and were sometimes called 'courting lamps' (the idea being that a gentleman could pay his court until the lamp ran out of fuel and then he had to leave). The earlier ones were very utilitarian, later ones more elaborately decorated and again, all forms of art glass could be used.

Miniature lamps were economical with fuel and could be used as night-lights for children or for courting couples, when subdued light was what was required.

Gas lamps

By the later nineteenth century gas lighting was the illumination of choice for many homes in heavily-populated urban areas. Early gas fixtures in the United States were mainly manufactured in England and France but by the middle of the century the US was producing a huge range of fixtures, elaborate chandeliers, sconces, newel post lamps, and portable table lamps in every imaginable style from Rococo to Arts and Crafts in finely cast and detailed bronze, brass and patinated white metal. You can still find many exquisite pieces with delicate glass shades.

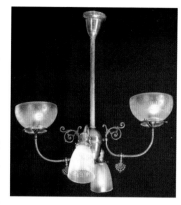

When electricity was first introduced, especially in the USA, the supply was often unreliable so many fittings were made for both gas and electricity, so if the electricity failed, at least you could still light the gas. This is a pretty example of a gas/electric fitting. (Photo: www.vintagelighting.com)

Portable gas lamps

'Portables' were table or desk lamps that received their gas by way of flexible rubber hoses connected to an outlet on a nearby wall. Portables were made in the shape of columns, vases or obelisks, often as classical figures such as cupids, soldiers or animals, each one holding the mantle and shade above its head. They might incorporate a cigar lighter as well as the light. The earliest burners had no shade and were like everlasting candles but these developed into open-ended globes with galleries that fitted under the burners. Later silk and parchment shades became popular but the burners had to be protected with glass or mica cylinders. Gas portables continued to be made until World War Two.

The continuously popular student's lamp and queen's reading lamp were also made as gas portables, complete with adjustable columns. The portables ranged in height from about 10 to 12 in, not counting the shade. They were usually fairly heavy so they couldn't easily be knocked over and always had upright burners.

Early electric lamps

In the late nineteenth and early twentieth century there was a huge variety from late Victorian, Art Nouveau, Arts and Crafts and Art Deco. There is no need to convert these, of course, although most will need to be rewired to conform to modern specifications. Electric table or side lamps could be made of a variety of materials. They could be chromed or made of brass, polished steel, silver plate or Bakelite.

Wall brackets

Kerosene/paraffin wall lamps were fixed to the wall by brass or cast-iron brackets so they were far enough away from the walls not to cause a fire. Some of these brackets had arms so the lamp could be swung in an arc to different positions. Cast-iron kerosene lamps in the nineteenth century often had double joints and many had hinged reflectors behind the lamp's glass chimney to aim light in different directions. Some brackets

A charming North American gas fitting is pivoted on a brass arm so that the light can be pointed further into the room and in various directions if required. (Photo: www. vintagelighting.com)

allowed two kerosene lamps to be mounted to the same fitting. A miniature wall lamp was made by various companies in which the bracket doubled as the reservoir for fuel, which often hung by a hook on the wall.

Early gas lamps of the late nineteenth century that were fixed to walls were known as gasoliers. Some had three arms, each with a fixture. The brass work on these brackets was often ornate and detailed with floral patterns and curlicues. The pipes that delivered the gas to the various lights on a fixture were often designed to look like slender vines or branches, while the keys that regulated the gas flow were cast to look like leaves or tassels.

Lampshades

Glass shades for paraffin/kerosene lamps

Glass shades provided a good opportunity for embellishment. Most shades were translucent, either frosted or coloured, and were often extremely ornate with cut glass decoration or etched patterns.

During the 1870s and 80s shades were usually large and globe-shaped with a slice taken off the top. Some were in clear glass; others were frosted, half-frosted or half milk glass and half clear. Ornament was added by acid etching (frosting) using stencils or by cutting a design into the glass. Etching was deep or shallow depending on how long the acid was left in contact with the glass. Often bolder patterns were cut and more intricate designs etched. Some shades were tinted or had colour at the edges. Others were hand-painted with images of flowers and birds and other designs, usually based on nature.

After the 1880s shades were made in a vast variety of shapes, often like sugar bowls or basins with scalloped or crimped edges. They might have thin wavy lines etched round the edges in close parallel lines and were often tinted pink, a feature called threaded ruby. When incandescent mantles were introduced with their fireproof glass chimneys, some had an additional opaline shade with frilly edges that sat over the chimney. Some had crystal and etched upright globes sitting on a gallery and extended over the chimney. Very wide globes both plain and decorated were used for lamps with cluster burners. Globes for out-of-door lighting were protected by wire cases that fitted over the glassware.

An English glass pendant shade made for electricity with orange and green decoration; probably 1930s. (Seen in Paul's Emporium)

Shades for gas lights

Shades for gas lights on the whole followed the designs of those for oil lamps, at least at first. They were produced in a variety of shapes and sizes and were usually made of clear glass, often with delicate etching. Gasoliers tended to have small shades ranging from a single glass bowl to a candle-shaped chimney to an upturned flower such as a lily. They were made in enormous quantities and great variety using clear or frosted, coloured, cut or etched glass, in a wonderful range of shapes from bell-shapes to frilly maid's bonnets, 'coolie-hat' shades, and daffodil-shaped shades. Cranberry, Vaseline and Nailsea glass were all popular. One type of gasolier had a nickel-plated brass 'oculist' bracket, which swivelled vertically as well as horizontally and took its name from its use by opticians to examine patients (it was also used by doctors and dentists).

Bowls on chains were attached to the central rod of single pendant gas lights and these prevented glare and diffused the light upwards to give background light for the whole room. They only worked in the way they were intended if the walls and ceiling were painted white or a pale colour, otherwise they would not reflect the light. Early bowls were dish-shaped and made of alabaster or milk glass. Later supastone glass (a brand made in Czechoslovakia) was used. Designs and patterns were either hand-painted or transfer printed. Some bowls were simply acid-etched to give a frosted look, or cut with intricate designs like the smaller shades. They ranged from 8in to 16in in diameter. During the 1920s bowls made of flakestone glass were cheap and became popular. They were marbled and were sold in many colours.

Shades for electric lights

For the first time, after electricity was introduced, wall lamps could have shades instead of just a chimney. Shades could now point down or up instead of just up, lighting the room in a more sophisticated way than paraffin/kerosene could achieve. They could be designed to fit in with different décors and could be made of materials other than glass such as parchment, silica and silk. One of the most fascinating periods for electric wall lights was Art Deco when the light source could be completely hidden by the shade.

Beaded shades

In the late 1920s beads of every kind became fashionable on clothes and bags and also on decorative domestic objects. Painted glass lampshades were trimmed with 3in or 4in glass bead fringes on single-stem glass pendants. Smaller beaded shades were used on swan-neck scroll brackets and on two-

If you were celebrated and famous, the Café de Paris in London was the place to go for an evening out in the 1930s. It was refurbished in the 1990s with reproductions of the original lights. This one is a table lamp with fabulous fringes.

or three-armed inverted pendants. Tiny beads were used to make intricate patterns of flowers, birds, garlands and bows which sparkled in the daylight, not just at night when the lights were lit. Large and small beads could be mixed to make interesting patterns.

Silica and parchment shades

Also called mica or 'Vitreosil' shades, these were standard cheaper shades for use with wall brackets. They were made of unbreakable heat-resistant silica and looked very like glass with a slightly streaky white appearance giving a pleasantly milky glow when lit. They had no etching or painted designs but were left quite plain. They were often fairly stocky in shape with a flange or crimped edge at the bottom.

In the 1920s and 30s mock vellum, parchment and early forms of plastic were used for lampshades on both pendant and table lamps. These were made in panels stitched together with cord or ribbon and trimmed with silk or bead fringing or tassels. Wooden or plastic beads, which were cheaper, might be used instead of glass. Like silk shades, they had to be used with protectors.

Silk shades

Victorian and Edwardian silk shades for gas lamps were highly elaborate. Some pendant lights had a 9in or 10in diameter brass band suspended from the gas pole. A silk flounce, weighted with a 2in beaded fringe, was threaded onto a piece of wire which fitted inside this band. Alternatively larger beads might be sewn round the edge at intervals to look like tassels. Sometimes the flounce was made up entirely of beads and sometimes the silk material was overlaid with lace ribbons, garlands or artificial flowers.

After World War One shades became much simpler but were still

This bedroom wall lamp gas fixture was made by the William Sugg Company in England. It has a fabric shade and a downward directed light. (Photo: Chris Sugg)

The Victorians liked luxurious fabric, generous bulbous shapes and fringes. This green silk lampshade has them all and the green colour would subdue the light so it wasn't too bright.

often trimmed with beads or bead fringing. Sometimes unweighted silk fringing was used instead of beads, presumably because it was cheaper. Many were intended for use on rise-and-fall lamps and were fashionable for hanging over a dining table. These were particularly popular in Britain, whereas in the United States moulded or blown glass shades were more popular. When beaded or silk shades were used on gas lamps the burners had to be protected with simple glass or mica fireproof globes or cylinders.

Smoke bells

Smoke bells for oil lamps became popular, with good reason, during the nineteenth century. They were designed to hang above a lamp to catch all the soot and smoke that would otherwise mark the ceiling. It was much easier to take down the smoke bell and wash it than to try to scrub the ceiling clean. Smoke bells came in all sorts of different shapes and sizes. There were large thistle-shaped bells, small flower-shaped bells and open bells like little mob caps. They could be made of clear, milk, acid-etched or coloured glass such as amberine, and quite a lot were made of stamped brass or enamelled steel or iron. Glass bells were sometimes given the rather pompous title of 'ceiling smoke consumers'.

This pendant paraffin/ kerosene lamp would have been designed for a library or parlour. It has brass fittings, a smoke bell and a pretty pink glass shade with a fringe.

Sometimes they were sold as separate accessories and sometimes they formed part of the whole design of a lamp. Upright incandescent mantles which were protected by mica glass chimneys could be fitted with a variety of smoke tops in porcelain, aluminium or brass. They were cone or crown-shaped and clipped onto the chimney with one or two clips or a circular gallery. They never completely covered the top but had a hole in the centre, at the sides of a pierced pattern to allow the gases from combustion to escape. Some fittings had china or enamel deflectors which fitted above the burners and inside the gallery which helped to deflect the heat and light away from the burner.

Art Nouveau

Art Nouveau really took over from the endless revival styles of the Victorian age – styles such as Neo-classical, Neo-Gothic, Renaissance and so on – and offered a completely new way of treating lighting, encouraged by the use of electricity. It was perhaps the first style to stop looking back in history for style ideas and to take its inspiration from the natural world around it.

In America most Art Nouveau lamps were made of opalescent glass and copper foil. Tiffany was the acknowledged master of this technique and his designs dominated all the art glass lighting in America at the time, to an extent that other lighting designers and manufacturers are inclined to disappear into the shadows. All the same, there were many other manufacturers producing wonderful lamps in the same manner using similar designs and many of these lamps can still be found all over the United States and Canada.

The very name Art Nouveau indicated a wish to think differently, to use materials differently, to design completely integrated interiors. Harmony was the Holy Grail and

Tiffany was the pioneer of exquisite art glass table lamps but copies abounded. Some were poor imitations but many were beautiful and indeed, many people who set up their own businesses had previously worked for Tiffany.

everything, from the architecture of a building to the colour and shape of its furnishings and even the handles and escutcheons on its doors – everything – had to match and co-ordinate. Architects found themselves designing not just buildings or the furniture in the buildings, but even the jardinières and certainly the lighting that went into these buildings.

The essence of Art Nouveau is in its sinuous, sensuous elongated lines and subtle light, feminine figures in pre-Raphaelite poses with their abundant curly hair, floating dresses, and natural curves, but also in controlled lines, geometric details, and colourful new shapes. New materials were used and combined, such as metal and glass or wood. Stylised flowers, leaves, roots, buds and seedpods were influenced by new botanical research.

Art Nouveau artists shared a belief in fine craftsmanship and quality materials. These included exotic woods, marquetry, iridescent glass, silver and semi-precious stones. The creators of Art Nouveau wanted to offer a modern way of life, to invent new shapes and free lines, to form one unique work of art, a total and harmonious artistic environment with no division between decorative art and fine art. This search for unity became the goal of Art Nouveau in all its manifestations among which was, importantly, electricity.

The advent of electricity, still new and extraordinary, meant that every designer wanted to design electric lights of some sort. Suddenly, from the days when you carried your light with you from room to room, lights were required permanently in every room and the whole question of how to light a room and what individual lamps should be like became a major preoccupation.

Tiffany lamps

Louis Comfort Tiffany was born in 1848. His father was founder of the well-known jewellery firm Tiffany & Co. As a young man he studied art in New York and Paris. While he was in France he met Emile Galle who was a botanist, producing art glass in Nancy. Tiffany was much influenced by his work which was very much based on nature, and by the Art Nouveau movement

The dragonfly motif was one of Tiffany's most popular designs. Whether you find an original Tiffany or a good copy, you will have a beautiful design and glowing colours.

which was just taking hold in Europe. When he returned to America after a period of painting he founded Louis Comfort Tiffany and Associated Artists in 1875. Here he employed over 100 skilled craftsmen on interior design schemes for well-off clients. He soon became the most fashionable decorator in New York, designing everything in each scheme in meticulous detail. Tiffany lamps became popular at home and abroad. From the beginning he used glass extensively together with tiles, murals, windows and lamps, as part of his altogether sumptuous designs that included influences from the Orient.

The lamps were made of tiny pieces of glass set in patterns with flowers, butterflies, dragonflies, spiders' webs, dogwoods, peacock feathers, flowers and other themes from nature. They had bronze bases and leaded shades. Later shades were sometimes made in folds from pressed glass panels with the appearance of a rough weave. The incandescence of Tiffany's Favrile glass shades was due to the light rays being intercepted and trapped by the opalescent glass so as to highlight its luminosity. The effect was magical indeed, but only those rays that escaped downwards were of any practical use for working or reading.

Tiffany-style art glass lamps were not just made as table lamps but could be floor-standing as well as in this one, set behind an easy chair to cast light downwards perhaps onto a book or needlework.

At first he used glass from outside companies but as his fascination with glass grew he experimented with lustre techniques of his own devising. He developed a unique process of formulating glass that could create bolder colours, opalescent sheens, and a wide range of textures. He patented four new types of glass over a twenty-year period.

Tiffany lamps were designed to the highest standards. Each glass piece was cut to precisely the correct size and each piece was soldered to the next one creating one large weld that encompassed the entire shade. After the soldering was finished, the shade was cleaned meticulously of dust and solder to ensure the brightest colours possible. Tiffany's passion for perfection meant that he did not in fact make a profit and ultimately his company became bankrupt.

The Tiffany technique:

- A model of the lampshade was first carved in wood.
- This was covered in glue and paper, or linen was laid over the form.
- The design was drawn onto the paper or linen, defining the different coloured areas of the chosen design, each of which would eventually be made of a separate piece of glass.

Tiffany lamps – did you know?

- Tiffany lamps were designed either by Tiffany himself or by artists working under his supervision. The bases of his lamps were usually in the form of fine sculptures using bronze. The shades were created by fitting hundreds of hand-cut coloured glass shapes into copper foil enclosures. Copper foil is light and strong so he was able to make large shades of complex design. Every lamp and shade was assigned a model number. Often inspired by the iridescence of ancient Roman glass. He patented this technique in 1881.
- Favrile glass was the trademark for Tiffany's hand-made glass and was the result of his own experiments and what he is best known for, apart, of course, from his lamps. The term 'Favrile' means handcrafted and is associated mainly with the early and simplest shades made by Tiffany himself. When he obtained his early patent under the name Favrile it included several types of glass used in the manufacture of stained glass windows as well as leaded and blown shades. Favrile pieces are usually inscribed L.C.T. or Favrile, whereas shades made from leaded glass are labelled with impressed metal signature tags.
- Tiffany lamps can be grouped into the following categories: irregular upper and lower border lamps, Favrile lamps, geometric lamps, transition to flowers lamps, flowered cone lamps, flowered globe lamps, irregular lower border lamps. The geometric lamps included such standard geometric shapes as squares, triangles, rectangles, ovals, ellipses and rhomboids used in panel, cone and globe-shaped shades.

- The paper or linen was removed from the wooden model and cut along the lines of the design to create a two-dimensional pattern.
- Each separate area was numbered and a copy made by tracing the design onto a separate piece of paper.
- The original was then cut into separate pieces along the drawn lines and each piece used as a template for the stained glass.
- When all the tiny glass pieces had been cut, adhesive was applied to the wooden model and the design laid out according to the copied plan, each piece being pressed into the adhesive wax to hold it in place until the whole thing was assembled.
- The pieces of glass were then removed one by one, edged with copper foil and soldered in place. The wooden model was heated to melt the wax, the lampshade removed and the inside edges of each glass piece soldered. Additional metal trim could be soldered to the top and bottom edges of the shade.

It is scarcely surprising that these original Tiffany lamps are so sought after and so difficult to get hold of. Many of them are already in museums and anyone who owns one is unlikely to want to get rid of it.

Some influential Art Nouveau/Arts and Crafts lamp designers

This elegant glowing table lamp is typical of those made by Handel & Company in Connecticut who made lamps similar to Tiffany's.

Behrens, Peter (1868–1940): German artist and designer. Director of the School of Arts and Crafts in Düsseldorf and artistic adviser to AEG in Berlin among many other appointments. He produced several iconic lights including the *Jugendstil* table lamp (1902); the *Luzette* pendant lamp in glass, copper and brass (c.1910); the AEG workshop lamp (1920s).

Benson, William Arthur Smith (1854–1934): British Arts and Crafts designer and manufacturer. Used a variety of materials including brass, copper, steel or bronze. His designs incorporated clean, simple lines but do have a traditional look.

Brandt, Edgar (1880–1960): French artist ironsmith, who at the age of 20 was already exhibiting exciting designs for lamps and chandeliers. His iron chandeliers incorporated botanically-inspired designs with leaves and buds, berries and tendrils, eucalyptus leaves and maidenhair ferns. The glass for his designs was often made by Daum Frères of Nancy or Sabino of Paris. He had a gallery in Paris and another in New York.

Caussé, Julien (1869–1914): French sculptor known for his small bronzes of women and flowers, and who designed several sculptural lamps in bronze, marble, stone and pewter with mythological or allegorical titles of young women with electric bulbs housed around the head or body.

Chalon, Louis (1866–1940): French sculptor who made a number of lamps, usually depicting half-naked nymphs or naiads bearing torches or enveloped in flowers whose petals house the electric bulbs.

Follet, Paul: French designer commissioned in 1901 to design light fittings for *La Maison Moderne* in Paris, mainly in chased bronze and stained glass. In 1923 was appointed director of Pomone, the art studio of Bon Marché; also created lamps in partnership with Edgar Brandt and Daum Frères.

Freshel, Curtis: US designer of leaded glass shades for Tiffany around the 1900s.

Guimard, Hector: French designer who designed many light fittings in both Art Nouveau and Art Deco styles spanning the late 1800s and early 1900s.

Gurschner, Gustav: Austrian sculptor working in Vienna and Paris in the late 1900s; designed anything from candlesticks to female nudes holding glass globes mostly in bronze with coloured patinas.

Hoffman, Josef (1870–1956): Austrian architect; founder of the *Wiener Werkstätte*. He designed some interesting lamps in the *Jugendstil* style.

Horta, Victor (1861–1947): Belgian architect and designer of lighting fixtures designed specifically for the interiors into which they were to go. Many still remain in their original settings; his lamps were often in the form of floral bouquets, with writhing tendrils and electric bulbs as the flower centres.

Laporte-Blairsy, Leo (1867–1923): French sculptor, one of the first artists to see the numerous design possibilities of electric lighting. His lamps were illuminated sculptures of luminous fantasies and *femme-fleur* themes depicting the naked female form together with flowers.

Larche, François-Raoul (1860–1812): French painter and sculptor who designed a range of illuminated sculptural light fittings; perhaps he is most famous for his illuminated sculptures of the dancer Loïe Fuller who became world famous for her 'light' dances.

Mackintosh, Charles Rennie (1868–1928): Scottish architect who believed in an integrated environment for his architecture and interior design. His light fittings were always designed to complement a particular room; materials included sheet metal and brass, often inset with panels of coloured glass.

Marjorelle, Louis (1859–1926): French sculptor known primarily for furniture, but also designed light fixtures with the metal bases mostly of ormolu, bronze or wrought iron, made in his own metal workshop in Nancy. The glass for his lamps came from Daum.

Rateau, Armand-Albert (1882–1938): French wood sculptor producing very individual pieces of great elegance, particularly lighting; influenced by eastern and ancient art.

Riemerschmid, Richard (1868–1957): German architect, painter and designer, founder member of the *Vereinigte Werkstätten* in Munich in 1898 which promoted the *Jugendstil* movement; created many table and ceiling fittings.

Van de Velde, Henry Clemens (1853–1957): Architect, interior designer and painter who was influenced by William Morris and the Arts and Crafts movement. He directed the Arts and Crafts School in Weimar from 1906–14. He designed a wide range of light fittings in the Art Nouveau style, for oil, gas, electric lights and candles.

Promoting the new lighting

To begin with, designers tended simply to adapt previous designs for oil and gas lamps to electricity and there seemed to be a dearth of any sort of creative thinking for the new form of lighting. In its April issue of 1898, *Art et Décoration* announced an electric lamp competition. It stipulated what was required: a two-bulb table or desk lamp on a cast copper base, the bulbs to be sheathed in shades to shield the glare… with a first prize of 79 francs. The jury found that the entries had all to some degree misunderstood the aesthetic aims of the competition, and no first prize was awarded. More competitions followed; again in 1898 *Art et Décoration* ran a competition for an electric suspension for a dining room and in 1904 another for a table lamp. *L'Art Décoratif pour Tous* (a supplement of *L'Art Décoratif* which was published briefly between 1902 and 1904) ran various competitions for gas, oil and electric lights in wrought iron and semi-precious metals (*orfèvrerie*) and *L'Art Décoratif* in 1906 invited readers to submit designs for an antechamber lantern. Numerous articles were written on lighting at the time. It became fashionable to find fault with contemporary lamp designs.

This beautiful cut glass pendant with its corolla of brass sepals would have looked good in almost any environment. It is both simple and intricate. (Photo: Antique Lighting Company)

The Paris International Exposition

The year 1900 was not just the birth of a new century but also the coming of age of electricity and the Paris International Exposition was an extraordinary celebration of both events. The Palace of Electricity at the exhibition was like something out of a fairy tale. The Palace itself was designed by architect Jean Renard. The lines of the building were picked out by thousands of coloured electric bulbs and the vast galleries inside showed both the latest achievements of industrial technology that were powered by electricity and sections on electric bulbs and lamps. The most amazing display of all was a magical fountain of water and light called the Château d'Eau in which water sparkled and streamed, lighting up a group of statues appearing like living stalactites. The wide range of modern electric lamps inside the Palace and in other displays throughout the grounds boosted the idea of electric lighting as something totally modern, wonderful and desirable.

New designs for a new century

Everyone, from architects and designers to artists, sculptors, ceramicists, glass-workers and craftsmen in metal and wood seems at some stage to have designed an electric lamp, whether chandelier, floor lamp, table lamp or ceiling lamp. The philosophy of an integrated design for the home in which, just as different rooms required different types of furniture, every room required some form of permanent electric lighting and the questions of how bright the light should be, how shaded, how directed were just beginning to intrigue people. Many of the lamps designed at the time were more useful as decorative objects than as lamps to see by.

In spite of the wish to co-ordinate the architecture and the furnishings there was still a tendency to create objects of beauty using light, rather than to create a new way of providing light. In fact perhaps one of the main features of Art Nouveau is its non-functionalism. It must be remembered that people were accustomed to the comparatively dim light cast by lamps of the past created by oil, paraffin/kerosene and candles, and many people found the new electric light blindingly bright and dazzling. In general Art Nouveau lamps generated more heat than light.

An opportunity for sculptors

Prominent sculptors such as Raoul Larche, who might have considered it beneath them to work on such small objects, were intrigued by the problems set and could also benefit not so much from one-off commissions, but from royalties from mass-production of their works from a large middle class beginning to incorporate electric lights into their homes.

In lamps as in other Art Nouveau designs the same range of themes was used: floral, botanics and entomological motifs and the figures of women. The designs of Charles Rennie Mackintosh in Glasgow were austere and spare with long vertical lines; in Paris whiplash curves and figures of women were popular. The insect world featured in the form of the praying mantis, the cicada, and the stag beetle crawling across lampshades; peacocks featured on table lamps but the most frequently used motifs were flowers. Plant life seemed ideally suited to the whole idea of electric light. The base formed a stem which carried the electric wire up to the flower head with its calyx and petals. Tiffany's Wisteria lamp became a wisteria tree and everybody loved it. Flowers that featured in lamps included poppies, cyclamen, hydrangea, honesty, and even cow parsley.

The other major theme was the nubile maiden released from constricting garments and sculpted as a caryatid supporting the lamp shade or holding a torch to herald the new century or clasping some object wired for electricity. The naked female form appeared everywhere on lamps, frequently together with flowers and was known as *femme-fleur*.

More nineteenth-century lamp fashions

Arts and Crafts

Like the Arts and Crafts movement in general, this was a Victorian style inspired by the belief that mass production belittled the worker and diminished the product. The style has much in common with Art Nouveau and occurred at much the same period, particularly in its belief in using good materials and craftsmanship but it differed in its aim for simplicity and geometric straight lines; the favoured materials were often iron, wood and stained glass.

Miniature fairy lamps

A less well-known fashion in the late nineteenth century was the huge variety of candle-burning fairy lamps or night-lights. They were popular in Victorian times, being the only type of lamp that was safe to leave burning in a room whether there was someone there or not. They consisted of a glass saucer to hold the candle and a glass cone with a hole in the top to enclose it. In England they were sometimes known as burglars' horrors because they scared away thieves who could never be sure whether there was anybody home or not if a dim light was left shining in a window. They were also safe to leave in the room of a child frightened of the dark and wouldn't blow out if you carried one up the stairs to bed.

An English stained glass lantern from the eighteenth century has an Arts and Crafts look of great charm and integrity. (Photo: Antique Lighting Company)

There were endless designs of fairy lamps and a broad range of art glass materials in pastel shades including satin glass, frosted glass, Nailsea glass (also called *verre-moiré*), crystal, lithophanes, cameo designs and Burmese glass, a peach-coloured satin glass with a floral decoration of which Queen Victoria was fond. There were bases similar to plain saucers or with crimped edges, others shaped like leaves, or eggcups. The best-known were marketed by Samuel Clarke, an English candle-maker who sold the holders to encourage sales of his candles. He never actually made any fairy lights, but patented those made by other manufacturers, granting licences to many glass and porcelain manufacturers in the UK, Europe and the United States to make lamp parts for his company. His patented lamps came in three sizes (fairy, pyramid and wee) each with a dome and matching lamp saucer. In 1910 Clarke's was taken over by Price's Patent Candles of London.

Fairy lamps were exported to America and were also made there, probably during the 1870s and 80s. Because they are sturdy little objects, there are many still around in enormous variety and many people like to collect them. If a night-light saucer has lost its dome or vice versa, the chances are that, in time, you may find another piece which will match.

Advice for householders on early electric lighting

There was no shortage of advice for householders on what lighting to choose and how to use it. To ensure proper lighting for various needs, it was recommended that homemakers keep a shelf of lamps, including a reading lamp, lamps with handles for carrying, and broad-bottomed metal kitchen lamps that did not tilt.

Recommendations for levels of light

The problem with early electric light was not that it was too dim, but that it seemed too blindingly bright. In *The Decoration of Houses*, an influential handbook by Edith Wharton and Ogden Codman which appeared in 1897, lighting is hardly mentioned, something unthinkable in any present-day book on decoration of homes. However, the authors did state that for the drawing room

A cosy converted room where the hosts have decided to rely mostly on candles. Would this have been considered too bright in the early twentieth century?

> Electric light, with its hard white glare, which no expedients have as yet overcome, has taken from our charming rooms all air of privacy and distinction…that such light is not needful…is shown by the fact that electric bulbs are usually covered by shades of some deep colour in order that the glare may be kept as inoffensive as possible.

They also thought that electric light made 'the salon look like a railway station, the dining room like a restaurant'. Candles, however, they considered brought out the subtle modellings of light and shade 'to which old furniture and objects of art owe half their expensiveness'.

Recommended levels of light

Recommended levels of illumination at the time (e.g. a 16 cp lamp was considered by one adviser to be adequate to light a room 10ft x 10ft) would be considered dismally ill-lit by today's standards. Gas lighting was still favoured by many people over electricity and the gas industry was still fighting back. In September 1898 *The Journal of Gas Lighting* commented that 'One big consumer after another grows tired of the costly little lamps with filaments that glow like newly burnt-out matches, the while his neighbour and rival makes a blaze with incandescent gas burners.' If the 16 cp lamps were too dim for comfort, the 8 cp lamp which was cheaper to buy and used less electricity was tempting but in fact provided an even dimmer light. Perhaps this is why so many of the original electric incandescent carbon lamps were not shaded, partly to show off the new technology and partly because shading the lamps would reduce what was already a poor light, especially if only a few lamps were used and the voltage was too low. Candlelight was still preferred for entertaining.

As a result of using unshaded lamps, many consumers complained of eye strain and headaches and opinion was divided as to whether electric lighting was intrinsically damaging to eyesight. A *Punch* cartoon of 1889 showed a group of ladies listening to a piano recital, each holding a highly fashionable Japanese parasol to protect them from the electric lights – a double dig at the fashion for all things Japanese and all lights electric. The advice against

A Victorian lamp with a barley-sugar twist wooden stem and a fringed Victorian silk shade nicely complements a Victorian chair and storage lockers.

the use of overhead lighting was particularly needed by wealthy householders who could afford the luxury of shaded table and standard lamps, recreating the pools of light once provided by candles and oil lamps. When 32 cp tungsten bulbs were introduced, shades became essential as light was not only brighter but also of a completely different quality, much whiter than the yellow colour produced by carbon filaments.

Candlelight was also still considered the best way of bringing sparkle to a party in the late nineteenth century. According to Wharton and Codman:

> No ball-room or salon is complete without its chandeliers: they are one of the characteristic features of a gala room (rooms used exclusively for entertaining). For a ballroom, where all should be light and brilliant, rock-crystal or cut glass chandeliers are most suitable, reflected in a long line of mirrors, they are an invaluable factor for any scheme of gala decoration.

One of the attractions, of course, was the way the mirroring would reflect light coming in through the windows and also at night the flickering of candles and chandeliers, of cut glass, prisms and droplets. Even towards the end of the nineteenth century people were used to such limited lighting that Wharton and Codman still considered that: 'the proper lighting is that of wax candles.'

Shading for electric lamps

However, although many people were not yet ready for the new electric light, it was beginning to find its way into many better-off homes by the late 1800s and some were embracing the idea with enthusiasm. How to deal with the new type of light, which was brighter and brasher than what people were used to, was a problem that people were beginning to tackle and there were books both practical and design-oriented, to help people who wanted to fit their home out with electric lights.

A ceramic lamp with a fabric shade; large fabric shades in old-fashioned styles are available to go with antique and vintage lamps.

Prismatic shades

By 1883 shades were being produced according to scientific principles that both protected the eyes and enhanced and diffused the light without much loss of illumination. In 1895 a 'dioptric' shade was introduced which enclosed the light source in a glass shade made up of several prisms. Originally these prismatic glass shades were designed for arc lamps but they were later introduced as a new invention by Blondel and Psaroudaki who founded their Holophane Company to sell it. After the introduction of tungsten bulbs Holophane shades became increasingly popular and were advertised in promotional literature sent out by electricity supply companies. Holophane shades were continually being updated and redesigned and remained popular in Britain up to the beginning of World War Two. They were also used in many factories.

W.A.S. Benson, a leading light in Arts and Crafts design and architecture and a pioneer of the new lighting industry, published *Notes on Electric Wiring and Fittings* in 1897. He provided comprehensive schemes for planning and wiring houses such as Standen in the south of England, an Arts and Crafts House designed by Philip Webb and built in 1893 (now owned by the National Trust). At Standen several of Benson's distinctive adaptable lights, which could be hung on a wall or set on a table, still survive and so do the hanging lights in the hall and stairway with their straw-opal streaked glass shades. At the same time, he also designed paraffin/kerosene lamps for Standen, an indication of how very new electricity still was for most people.

Decorative Electricity by Mrs J.E.H. Gordon set itself the task of advising on electric lighting throughout the home. Mrs Gordon was married to an electrical engineer who was responsible for the first electric lighting installed at Paddington Station in 1886

Decorative electric lighting

Electric light was used not just to see by but for highly inventive displays. In America one of the first people to use electric light for personal adornment was Mrs Cornelius Vanderbilt who in 1883 had an 'Electric Light' ball-gown in blue velvet and satin designed by Worth. It had a little battery concealed in the bodice 'which did not interfere with dancing in the least'. There was electric jewellery, often in the form of scarf pins and lapel decorations, and even electric tablecloths which were effective as long as nobody spilled their wine on the cloth, in which case there was a rush to mop it up in case the moisture short-circuited the cloth and blew all the fuses.

There were electric candlesticks that could be pronged into the tablecloth and other ornamental fixtures such as 'quaintly illuminated insects…and flowers and fruit'. Mrs Gordon, the wife of a British electrical engineer, was one of the first to wear electric jewels. She described some of the perils in her 1891 book of advice for householders, *Decorative Electricity*:

Sometimes the battery heated, and leaked, and once I well remember, the old lamps having worn out, I had some new ones given to me that were a wrong resistance for the battery. It heated, and we barely had time to cast the battery into the bath before the gutta-percha sides gave way, and the acids poured out, taking off all the paint. So having spoilt a dress, a carpet, and a bath, I abandoned personal electric light decorations.

She also suggested that 'growing strawberry plants look charming with little lights beneath their leaves; so do dwarf orange and lemon trees, the fruit scooped out and the lamps hung inside the empty rinds'.

and surrounding streets. When they were first married, she used to help her husband in his workshop so she had a good understanding of the technology and also of the effects that electric lighting could achieve:

'So far,' she wrote in her book, 'designers of electric light fittings are too much the slaves of precedent, derived from their experiences with gas, candles, oil, and other relics of the Middle Ages, forgetting that the shapes of the holders of all these lights are determined by the necessity of leaving a clear space above the flame for the escape of hot and foul air, and also by the condition that they must be within reach of the taper or match used for lighting them.'

Her book takes a tour round the whole house, advising on different lighting for each room, and crucially for the 'servants' departments' (and also the bedrooms of the younger maids, where the light should be controlled from a switch in the housekeeper's room so that they wouldn't waste electricity by keeping the lights on too long).

Mrs Gordon was way ahead of her time in her understanding of the way light can be used when you don't have to worry about a flame:

> For the drawing room I believe that, whatever the illuminant used, the light of the future will be a reflected light. What we have to aim at is, that the room should be flooded with a warm, soft radiance and that we should be unconscious of the source from which it proceeds.

A characteristic use of glass globes, albeit rather more decorative than the popular plain round globe, here used as outside lighting.

At first the types of electric lights available all looked rather similar to the paraffin/kerosene oil lamps that had gone before. The different fuels were in strong competition with each other. So a standard lamp would be of uniform design, whether it was for gas, oil or electricity. The support was usually telescopic in iron, brass or wood with an elaborate silk shade all shiny and fringed. Clusters of wall and ceiling lamps looked like a bunch of flowers with etched, frilly and coloured shades. Many candle, oil or gas fittings were adapted and new ones were made in late seventeenth- and early eighteenth-century styles. Early electric lights had to be made to look user-friendly and not too uncompromisingly modern.

By the 1930s, electricity had become much cheaper and there was enormously increased consumption so a range of light fittings had to be produced in order to cope with demand. Simple cardboard or fabric shades were still common, more sophisticated table lamps on vase bases and shaded in vellum, parchment or pleated silk gave a soft light for sitting rooms. Indirect lighting was concealed in more formal drawing rooms by being positioned at intervals behind the cornice. Although neon lighting was available in the 1930s it was rarely used in most homes until much later. Modern functional glass and chrome shades gave a clear light for hallways, kitchens and bathroom.

Advice in women's magazines

By the 1920s advice on home lighting was a required subject in women's magazines. The February 1925 issue of *Good Housekeeping* in the United States explained how important it was that light should not cast shadows over the work surfaces in the kitchen.

However, at this time much thought was going into the design of lamps themselves which became as decorative as valuable vases. A lamp might have a ceramic base made in Germany covered in cupids and tiny rosebuds in pink and white with an etched glass globe as its shade. Glass shades were available in pineapple shapes and embossed finishes, with curly edges and two-tone colours.

World War One interrupted this burgeoning of decorative lighting and the next chapter will look at the burst of creativity that followed it and then what followed after the domestic design doldrums of World War Two when a very different approach was taken to illuminating not just the home, but the outside environment as well.

CHAPTER THREE

Twentieth Century – Lighting for a New Age

Early twentieth century

Goodbye to Art Nouveau

World War One created a chasm between the ideas and designs of the nineteenth century and the turn towards modernism with its view of a new and different approach to life. Art Nouveau had reached its high point at the 1902 Turin International Exposition and by 1913 it was coming to the end of its creativity. Where lighting was concerned, it was considered by the new post-war generation to be over-ornamented to such an extent as to disguise the fact that its purpose was actually to provide light. Some designers thought that if the purpose of light was to illuminate rooms and objects, it should cease to be part of the decoration of the room. Electricity could now be used to light work stations in factories and factory lighting became a branch of lighting in itself, following the idea of 'form follows function'. Factory lights which once seemed so brutal and basic are now seen as elegant and functional and often perfectly acceptable as part of a domestic interior.

Designers of lamps had to decide whether to make their lamps as functional and unostentatious as possible or to do away with them altogether and find a way of lighting in which the light source was not seen. Lighting now began to be labelled according to what it was intended to do. Such terms as direct and semi-direct and indirect, for example, were used for different ways of directing light. Light fixtures remained, and invisible lighting arrived alongside them. An article in the lighting journal *Lux* of April 1928 suggested that 'It is an advantage to

This metal-shaded light is typical of the ideas of the new century, being practical, sturdy and easily mass-produced. Rows of lamps like these would have been used to illuminate a whole workshop.

hide the light source, as the effect is more striking when one cannot see its origin. Hence the disappearance of bulbs into walls, ceilings and behind pilasters where they were masked by diffuser screens.' Art Deco lighting, which became so universal between the two world wars, took on board all this thinking. One of its main characteristics was the opaque glass shade, usually white or pale pinks and buffs, which gave a shaped soft glow.

This big English Art Deco pendant glass shade is typical in its squared-off geometric shape and brownish-yellowy mottled colours. It was probably produced in the 1930s to hang in a family drawing room, or perhaps the dining room. It would have diffused and softened the light very effectively. (Seen in Paul's Emporium)

Since light was now so easy to acquire, plenty of thinking went into how to make best use of it. Alongside the sleek lines of everyday illumination epitomised by Art Deco, there were plenty of intriguing and frankly eccentric lamps. Some were specially produced to provide a background glow to television sets (this was supposed to be less of a strain on the eyes than watching a bright screen in a darkened room). There were lamps that made use of science to produce eerie effects (such as lava lamps, with their globular moving shapes) and other modern innovations. But at the turn of the twentieth century electric lighting in the home was still a rarity and turning on lights at the flick of a switch still seemed to many people something like magic

Loyalty to the mantle lamp

Things didn't change overnight for most people. Even as electricity was on the verge of becoming the primary source of domestic lighting, many people were still using paraffin/kerosene and new improvements were still being made to liquid fuel lamps. Arthur Kitson in Britain, one of the pioneers of pressure mantle lamps, designed and built a pressure-driven vapour-burning lamp in the mid 1890s but he didn't take out his US patent until 1898. The Kitson lamp is probably the best-known from that period in Europe. By 1920 he was claiming to be 'supplier of goods to the British and all other allied Governments in large quantities'.

Success of the pressure lamp

In 1909 the Mantle Lamp Company of America produced an incandescent kerosene light by heating a mantle without requiring it to be pumped like other fuel lamps to keep the fuel tank pressurised. It produced no smoke or odour and the light source itself did not flicker. This was the first Aladdin lamp and it quickly made the company famous. Aladdin's first lamps had tall glass chimneys and brass or nickel-plated bases.

Other pressurised lamp companies included Coleman lamps: W.C. Coleman was a typewriter salesman in 1899 but became interested in the 'Efficient Lamp' invented by W.H. Irby. Coleman formed his own company, the Hydro-Carbon Light Company, manufacturing a 'hollow wire' lighting system around 1905. In this the fuel was carried through a hollow copper wire from the fuel tank to the lamp. The first Coleman table lamp was launched in 1909, and was followed by the Air-O-Lite lamp and in 1914 by the first lantern.

This beautifully restored Coleman Quick-Lite pressure lamp was created in 1926 and has an elegant white glass shade that would make it eminently suitable for use in the home. (Photo: www.museum-of-pressurelamps.net)

Primus in Sweden, Coleman in America and Veritas, Tilley and Vapalux (Aladdin) in Britain made up a large part of the market in pressure lighting, although there were other companies producing such lamps too. Many North American Coleman pressure lamps were available for use with petrol as the fuel but they were never widely used in Britain – no doubt petrol was considered too dangerous.

Improvements in technology meant that by the early twentieth century every manufacturer of pressure lamps had incorporated a fine needle inside the vaporiser to clean the injector tip and either a spirit holder or 'roarer' to start paraffin lamps, and a small spirit cup or an 'instant light facility' to start petroleum lamps. The circular spiral vaporiser surrounding an inverted mantle was designed in 1931 by W.B. Engh and became the standard design for manufacturers such as Primus, Optimus and Graetz (makers of Petromax) and later for Coleman. Initially Coleman's method of achieving good evaporation of fuel oil was to use twin mantles either side of a vertical generator, virtually doubling the heat input into the oil and eliminating the shadow of the fuel bowl.

The English Tilley lamp became so popular that it became the generic term for pressure lamps in many parts of the world. This is an elderly Tilley waiting for an overhaul. Tilley are still making lamps and will still provide parts for antique examples, as do many of the original pressure lamp manufacturers.

Aladdin and its wonderful lamps

In 1926 Aladdin bought a company called Lippincott Glass which allowed it to manufacture its own chimneys, lampshades and bases. The vase kerosene lamps made from 1930 to 1935 had a removable brass fuel pot; the glass bases were easily chipped which makes an undamaged Aladdin vase lamp from this period difficult to find. These designs are still considered classics of the type. Aladdin produced many different designs of lamps, most of which are highly collectible today:

- Aladdin lamps included the Florentine, Venetian Art Craft and Venetian, Washington Drape and Simplicity, Victoria, Hopalong Cassidy, Aladex and others. Of these the Florentine was produced in moonstone glass in green, white or rose and the Venetian Art Craft lamps in colours ranging from blue to ebony. Later in the 1930s Aladdin introduced the Vertique line, named after the lamp's vertical ridges.
- In 1938 Aladdin introduced an ivory opalescent glass called Alacite, originally coloured with uranium. But in 1942, when uranium was reserved for the nation's war effort, a new formula was introduced called Opalique. The most popular Aladdin kerosene lamp ever made was the Alacite Lincoln Drape, which was manufactured throughout the 1940s.
- Aladdin did not start making electric lamps until 1930, an indication of how long it took for electricity to become the *sine qua non* of domestic lighting. By 1956 the company had made its last electric lamps. It continued to manufacture kerosene lamps in the United States out of brass imported from England until 1963. By 1977 all manufacturing had moved to Hong Kong and in 1999 Aladdin industries sold its legendary lamp division to a group of investors who renamed their business Aladdin Mantle Lamp Company and it still produces non-electric Aladdin lamps today.
- From a collector's point of view, the first Aladdin kerosene lamps made between 1909 and 1910 are the hardest to find, although Model 2 Aladdin lamps made between September and December 1910 are not too uncommon. From 1913 the model number was stamped on the lamp's wick-raising knob.

Art Deco lighting

The changes in thinking about light were first apparent with the advent of Art Deco. The style first made itself known at the 1925 *Exposition Internationale des Arts Décoratifs et Industriels Modernes* in Paris. It dominated architecture, furniture, domestic appliances, jewellery, graphic arts and transport right through the 1920s and 30s. The philosophy of the 1920s expressed itself in a number of parallel movements such as Jazz style and Modernist, and was the antithesis to Art Nouveau. It became the name under which all related movements were categorised.

The difference in lighting between Art Nouveau and Art Deco was very pronounced. Where Art Nouveau had relied on creating beautiful lamps out of exotic materials with intricate shapes and very bright lustrous colours, many Art Deco lampshades relied on effects other than colour for their impact. In place of beautifully coloured, patterned and shaped lamps, the leaning was towards simplicity of line, and direction of light.

White glass globes were a very popular form of shade for electric light in the 1930s, giving an efficient but not blinding light and the globes themselves were decorative, especially when used, as here, in rows to light a hallway, lobby or passage.

The materials, too, had begun to change. Bronze, so much used by the adherents of Art Nouveau, became less fashionable (although it was still used for mass-producing sculptural lamp bases). In its place were brand-new machine-age materials of the time, particularly chrome, plastic and aluminium as well as painted metal, alabaster, marble, lacquer, mirror and sharkskin – all things hard and shiny. Glass was sandblasted, etched or enamelled rather than coloured. New designers turned away from nature and took their inspiration from modern archaeological finds such as Tutankhamun's tomb in Egypt, and discoveries of Mayan and Aztec civilisations in South America, turning to geometric shapes and zigzags. They took many of their stylised images from modern technology and architecture such as aeroplanes, cars, cruise liners and skyscrapers. And these buildings were adorned and enhanced by lighting that reflected their own styles. Nature motifs included shells, sunrises and flowers but not in the sinuous Art Nouveau style. Art Deco was much more angular. Influences included cubism, Russian ballet and the glamour of early Hollywood films.

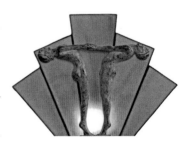

Many lamps were machine-made which offered more variety for the consumer. An athletic maiden in chrome, for example, a vision of the liberated woman of the day, might be turned out in various configurations so that the top half which held the globe in its silvery hands could be attached to various versions of the bottom half, so you could choose whether your maiden would be kneeling or standing. Pierrot and his consort Pierrette were popular emblems of the Art

This wall lamp with its naked female figures, its sharp geometric sunray design and subtly-coloured glass is typical of the Art Deco period.

Deco movement; romantic, sad and amusing all at the same time.

By the 1920s it was no longer considered enough to make a beautiful lamp; the light fixture had a specific job, to ensure a logical distribution of the light that would meet the requirements of visibility and ambience. Lamps became simply the vehicles for light to be distributed to wherever it was needed. This explains why Art Deco lamps often appear to be upside-down until it is understood that the function of the shade was to project the light onto the ceiling which in turn softens and diffuses it. In fact, the most popular lights in the 1930s were uplighters. They were usually made of concave glass in a semi-circular shape or of moulded or panelled glass in a metal frame. New cinemas, notably the Odeons, installed them in all their local picture-houses, helping to popularise this type of lighting.

Here's a charming Art Deco table lamp consisting of a girl holding a convolvulus flower which is directing the light upwards.

Spreading the light

Designers of both visible and invisible lighting had plenty of opportunity to create wonderful lamps. A 'Grand Competition of Light' was arranged in Paris in 1924 by the Syndicated Union of Electricity. In 1925 the *Exposition Internationale* provided another excellent showcase, and in the 1930s five Salons of Light were held.

And, of course, there were the annual Salons and the splendid ocean liners. Ships such as the *Normandie*, *Île de France*, *L'Atlantique*, *Empress of Britain* and the Swedish *Kungsholm* provided designers with opportunities to experiment with the most modern and stunning lighting effects. Of course, too, posh hotels, such as the Savoy in London and up-to-date theatres such as the Roxy Theatre and Radio City Music Hall in New York were showcases for the newest in electric light. Lighting became the talk of the town and by 1928 there were no fewer than fifteen journals devoted to the subject of lighting. The one most concerned with lighting and Art Deco was *Lux*, a monthly journal published in Paris to highlight developments in domestic and commercial lighting.

René Lalique, famous for his glass and his jewellery, studied at Sydenham Art College in London before

An Art Deco maiden holding a glass trumpet which is the source of the light. This lamp echoes the ideas in the previous lamp and is typical of the Art Deco period. It was produced by Frankart in the 1930s. (Photo: David Negley)

A 1930s European art glass pendant hanging in a conservatory. The glass has a slightly greenish tinge that softens the light and the pattern is deeply embedded.

An autumnal brown colour for this table lamp which is used for both shade and pedestal give this 1930s English lamp a gorgeous warm golden glow when lit. It would have been intended for a drawing room.

returning to Paris and his own jewellery workshop. He designed Art Nouveau pieces and later Art Deco. He was responsible for the walls of lighted glass and elegant glass columns in the dining room and grand salon of the SS *Normandie*.

Interior design styles often follow architecture closely. Following the streamlined Art Deco architectural masterpieces of the early twentieth century such as the Chrysler Building in New York, the Hoover Building in London and sculptural Art Deco homes built during the period between World War One and World War Two, interiors too became streamlined machines for living. The discovery of electric light meant there was a need to find new ways of dealing with light in general and Art Deco lighting fixtures provided many answers. In fact there was a sensuous side to Art Deco, especially in the lamps created during the 1920s and 30s in which nude female figurines stood or reclined next to illuminated glass globes. Many of these Art Deco lamps, on bases that ranged from alabaster to marble, were openly erotic, taking their visual cues from

A pyramidal shape for this Art Deco wall lamp acknowledges the archaeological finds being discovered in Egypt with echoes also of the amazing new skyscrapers being built in New York.

The Apotheosis of Light

Loïe Fuller was an American dancer. By 1892 she had moved to Paris, where she used coloured lights in her various illuminated stage performances at the Folies Bergère. She used these lighting effects and floating silk garments to extraordinary effect and became known as 'Loïe Fuller – Apotheosis of Light'. She held patents related to stage lighting including chemical compounds for creating colour gel and the use of chemical salts for luminescent lighting and garments.

She became the subject of numerous small sculptures, some of which incorporated hidden lighting. One or two designed by Raoul Larche are the best known although Clara Pfeifer, a compatriot of Loïe's also designed a charming table lamp based on the dancer, which she exhibited at the 1901 Salon of the *Société des Artistes Français*.

the showgirl culture of the Moulin Rouge in Paris. In spite of their erotic quality, the architectural style of clean lines and functional practical elements is reflected in these pieces.

The variety of materials and invention was enormous and many well-known designers tried their hand at devising lamps. Lamps could range from the whimsical Pixie lamps by A.R. Gerdago in which bronze harlequins played with millefiori globes or Enrique Mollins Balleste's female figurines in spelter which were gilded in silver or gold with globes of frosted glass.

In the United States Ronson Art Metal Works of New York produced Art Deco figural lamps with Egyptian themes. Ronson's Egyptian Moon lamp is one of many from the period to jump onto the Egyptian bandwagon. Some depicted Cleopatra herself. Even the Aladdin Company began to create Art Deco lamps with glass bases remarkably like those of Lalique. Other popular themes were animals such as gazelles or cobras or architecture such as stepped pyramids.

Pierrot was often used as a motif in lamps of the 1920s and 1930s. This one is in ceramic with a transparent white glass globe on his knees. The light illuminates his face from below. (Photo: Louise Verber at Alfie's Antique Market)

A design opportunity for sculptors

In design terms Europe was a hotbed of creativity during the late nineteenth and early twentieth century. Many of the most gifted designers of the time were working in Brussels and France and many took to designing lamps and lighting like ducks to water. After all, the possibilities of lighting, whether in streets, public places, workplaces or the home was suddenly offering unheard-of potential and opportunities.

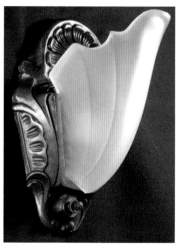

Sculptors feature prominently in Art Deco lamps because lighting fixtures in Europe around 1900 were made of a variety of materials including bronze. The use of bronze gave opportunities for sculptors and designers to create 'sculpted' forms for lamps, everyday household objects they would usually have considered well beneath them. Foundries began to produce more and more 'runs' of bronze lamps to meet the huge middle-class demand for more light – and more lamps. The manufacturers negotiated copyrights with well-known sculptors who were

This elegant wall lamp with a glass shell shade was designed in the USA as an uplighter. It is both elegant and understated and an excellent source for hidden light. (Photo: Vintage Lighting)

pleased to receive generous royalties on their work. Sculptors who benefited in this way from their lighting designs included Raoul Larche, Maurice Bonval and Ville Vallgren. Frankart Lamps' main sculptor and designer, Arthur von Frankenberg used to combine nude female figurines with skyscraper-inspired shades. Other American firms producing similar lamps include Ronson, Betty Beck and Nuart.

Some influential Art Deco designers

Adnet, Jacques: French artist who in the 1920s designed mainly chandeliers and desk lamps in stark geometrical designs, using a lot of nickel in his lively creations.

Argy-Rousseau, Gabriel: French glass artist prominent in the 1920s, specialising in *pâte-de-verre* and *pâte-de-crystal* glass. He produced small table lamps often with bases of wrought iron and shades in quiet russets, ochres and olive greens, with motifs of flowers or fruits against a lighter ground. His *pâte-de-crystal* statuettes had a light source in the base, not unlike those of Lalique or Sabino.

Bagues Frères: French partnership producing reproductions of antique light fittings, particularly Louis XIV and Empire styles using opalescent crystal beads – as well as Art Deco.

Bauhaus, Weimar, Germany: The Bauhaus was an art educational institute and design centre from 1919–33, founded by Walter Gropius. László Moholy-Nagy became director of the metal workshop in 1923 and for the next five years, along with his colleagues Max Krajewski and Marianne Brandt took a particular interest in developing lamps and light fittings in Art Deco styles using the new materials aluminium and chromium, often combined with opaque and matt glass or Bakelite.

Brandt, Edgar: (see under Art Nouveau/Arts and Crafts, p. 63)

Charreau, Pierre (1883–1950): French architect, decorator and designer who believed that an object's function should determine its shape. He designed table lamps and chandeliers in alabaster but was also one of the first to conceal lighting behind ceiling cornices.

Chiparus, Demetre H.: Romanian sculptor working in Paris during the 1920s, whose figure lamps were particularly influenced by the excavation of the Pharaoh's tombs in Egypt and by the Diaghilev Ballet.

Damon, France: Art Deco designer and manufacturer who made his own lamps and manufactured for other leading designers including Boris Jean Lacroix, Georges Martin and Daniel Stéphan. His own designs were intended to be functional with an elegant spareness using chrome, silvered bronze and nickelled copper. He developed a special glass, enamelled on the inside and frosted on the outside, called *verre émaillé diffusant*, which was designed for perfect, even diffusion of light without glare. He used the glass in many of his lamps, framed with metal.

Desky, Donald: US designer who directed the interior design of the Radio City Music Hall, Rockefeller Center, New York. His light fittings used all the modern materials newly available, including aluminium, Bakelite and 'Vibrolite'. His shades were often of parchment or cloth.

D.I.M. (*Décoration Intérieur Moderne*): French lighting company founded by René Joubert in 1914. By 1930 it had become one of the largest studio galleries in Paris. They produced not only their own light fittings but also designs by other well-known artists.

Dufrene, Maurice: French designer who founded La Maîtrise studios at Galeries Lafayette which designed and produced a range of home furnishings for customers. Many well-known artists designed for La Maîtrise, including Jacques Adnet.

Dunaime, Georges: French lighting designer during the 1920s who produced many light fittings and won the contract to supply the light fittings for the ocean liner *Paris*. In 1924 he was awarded first prize for a 'table lamp for an average income home' at the Great Lighting Competition in Paris.

Etling, Edmond et Cie: French company that marketed a range of small chrome metal and crystal lamps designed by leading artists.

Frankart Inc.: US lighting company which produced a range of *femme-fleur* lamps and bronze-based table lamps depicting female nudes holding geometric glass shades.

Genet & Michon: French lighting company which produced table lamps, wall brackets, chandeliers and pendants but also illuminated ceilings, columns, cornices and friezes. They used a special pressed glass whose ingredients were kept secret.

Hagenauer, Karl: Austrian son of a metal engraver and master caster, who worked in his father's workshop from 1919, becoming a leading designer and manufacturer of Art Deco lamps in simple, curved lines.

Kohlmann, Etienne: French cabinetmaker and interior designer who produced a wide range of light fittings including in 1934 a series of Holophane fixtures.

Le Chevallier, Jacques: French artist who succeeded in many fields but he is particularly known for a range of very functional lamps and fittings.

Le Verrier, Max: French sculptor popular in the 1920s, known for depicting female figures holding a globe and also for a range of Pierrot lamps, ceiling fitments and chandeliers.

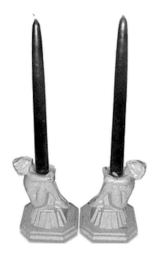

The Frankart Company in the USA produced a range of femme-fleur *lamps depicting female nudes – these little turquoise-coloured ceramic examples are in the form of candlesticks.* (Photo: David Negley)

An interesting pendant in mottled glass which seems to be hanging upside-down but it is designed to direct the light upwards to reflect off the ceiling and also to give a warm glow from the cone-shaped bowl. (Seen in Paul's Emporium)

Limousin: French sculptor of bronze or spelter figures of lithe girls, some made into lamps.

Lorenzl: Austrian sculptor who produced many Art Deco female figures in bronze and chryselephantine, some of which were turned into lamps.

Mallet-Stevens, Robert: French architect and furniture designer who designed integrated lighting systems for his buildings, choosing for preference modern materials such as chrome, aluminium and steel.

Moholy-Nagy, László: Hungarian, director of the metal workshop at the Bauhaus from 1923–28. He was particularly interested in developing lamps in simple Art Deco shapes, using modern materials such as chrome and aluminium with matt and opaque glass shades or panels.

Paris, Roland: Austrian sculptor of Art Deco figures and lamps.

Perzel, Jean: Bohemian glassmaker who worked in Paris from 1902 designing and manufacturing light fittings in modern, highly functional styles, designed to maximise while diffusing the light. Designed light fittings for many important state and royal buildings all over the world and for the luxury ocean liner SS *Normandie*.

Printz, Eugène: French designer who concentrated on architectural lighting effects that inspired other artists, and created concealed and visible lighting fixtures in Paris during the 1920s and 1930s.

Robert, Emile: French ironsmith who created all kinds of intricate and delicate light fittings and chandeliers, mainly for gas and oil lamps in forged or beaten iron with delicate clusters of flowers ending in tendrils for the light fittings.

Ruhlman, Emile-Joseph: French furniture designer who designed all kinds of light fixtures as well as architectural lighting. His wall brackets in bronze and alabaster were simple but luxurious.

A true retro classic, the Cubo was a small red plastic box which opened up to reveal a light bulb. The light switched on automatically when the lid was lifted. This Italian lamp, designed by Bettonica and Melocchi for Cini & Nils was popular in the 1960s as a symbol of all things new, coloured and fun. (Photo: *www. classic-modern.co.uk*)

Materials used in twentieth-century lighting

- Bakelite was one of the first synthetic plastics made from phenolic resin in 1907. At first it was a very hard and brittle material but with the addition of wood, flour or other fibres, it became more resilient and acquired a mottled appearance. It was used extensively in the electrical industry for lampholders, fitments, plugs and casings for lamps and radios, among many other household items.
- Brass.
- Bronze.
- Plexiglass, a light, transparent weather-resistant thermoplastic which was used in many lights in the second half of the twentieth century.
- Split pine was used in many Scandinavian lamps.
- Glass, in its many forms, continued to be used for the shades of many lamps.
- Enamelled metal provided a good, durable finish for many modern lamps.

The green shade desk lamp

Among the most enduringly popular of all the types of early desk lamp are those with an oblong green shade. Any film of the early twentieth century with an office in it would have had one of these lamps – that hallmark of the must-have desk lamp. These brass lamps with their green glass shades are often referred to as bankers' lamps. They were made by H.G. McFaddin & Co. in America under the names Emeralite and Bellova and the glass was ordered exclusively by McFaddin from J. Schreiber & Neffen in Czechoslovakia.

The first Emeralite lamp was launched in 1909 using the cased glass technique; the shades were made of white opal glass on the inside with a layer of green or blue glass on the outside. (In modern reproductions, the shade is usually green but blue was used as often as green in the originals.) The first shades were perforated with a hole at each side and the shade was attached to the very simple base through these holes and could be swivelled and locked into position. The most successful Emeralite lamps, the 8734 series, began production in 1916 and lasted until the early 1930s. The shade was clamped into the base, which was usually of solid brass with a hidden cast-iron weight at the bottom. The shade could be removed for cleaning

Desk lamps like this became symbols of what a business person's desk lamp should be with its angled head, coloured shade (usually blue or green); it was often called a banker's lamp.

or replacement without disturbing the concealed electric wiring. Models included lamps for desks, bedsides, floors, adding machines, side chairs, draughtsman's tables, typewriter tables and many other uses. They could also have optional removable inkwells, pen-holders and pens, clocks and calendars.

McFaddin introduced its Bellova shades in 1923. These were in many colours including russet brown, Rhodolite (marbled and opaque) chamois and rose, sometimes with an acid-etched texture or painted with an air-brush or reverse-painted by hand. Many of the Bellova shades available today will fit the Emeralite 8734 desk lamp but they were often given fancier bases than the usual models and were sometimes designed and painted specifically to complement the shade.

Other lamps made by the company were the Gnome lamps with a glass ball-shaped or cylindrical bottom with a mushroom or 'coolie-hat' glass top. The largest were called simply Gnome lamps, the medium ones, Miniature Gnomes and the smallest (about 4in tall) Petite Gnomes. The colours, acid-etched patterns and designs were numerous but most were either floral or geometric. Some Gnome lamps depicted children or animals playing, or oriental figures which were applied using transfers rather than being hand-painted. All Emeralite and Bellova shades were signed with an ink stamp or a decal.

Today you can find many reproductions of Emeralite and Bellova lamps, often sold as 'bankers' lamps', many made in China, usually with an antiqued brass finish.

Pan lights

Electric pendant pan lights were popular in the United States from about 1900 through to 1930 because of their low cost and simplicity, which made them suitable for many different situations. The fixture consisted of a shallow brass pan with a lid, suspended from a chain which was usually attached to an adjustable brass post emerging from a ceiling cup. Under the pan there were anything from two to five arms radiating outwards, each of which bore a light bulb. In most pan lights the bulbs were directed downwards. The fitting was either enclosed in a brass bell from which the glass shade hung, or there might be a wide collar and no shade. Any ornamentation came from the cast brass arms, which could be quite elaborate, and the central dangling finial which held the assembly together. The glass shades came in a wonderful variety of designs in pressed, etched, frosted and cut glass, in opaque, coloured glass, and in 'scenic' glass with flowers, fruits, buildings and other scenery.

Later twentieth-century

Post World War Two domestic lighting saw many changes in technology and design. Immediately after the war lighting was characterised by simple lines and a space-age feel. Folded and pleated paper shades from Denmark became fashionable – and were cheap. Designers made use of many materials and lamps were often made of metal or plastic as well as glass and wood. The angled desk lamp, originating from the Anglepoise, was an essential for drawing offices and home offices. There were gimmicky lights to emphasise the versatility of electricity like those that created moving pictures on the shades, and TV lights, to lessen eye strain from watching a bright screen in a completely darkened room. There were fun lamps and serious lamps, lamps that blended in with the architecture and lamps that made decorative statements while diffusing the light to very good practical effect.

Many curious new ideas and images were used for lamps, particularly as plastic made mass-production possible. This plastic pineapple is typical of the sort of lamp that could be cheap and fun. (Photo: Louise Verber at Alfie's Antique Market)

Individual designers began to produce innovative lighting using light and colour technology as well as new types of electric lighting systems. Many of the best design minds, working in co-operation with small, largely family-run firms meant that a flood of new ideas and lighting designs came pouring out of Europe, in particular from Italy and Scandinavia but also from Germany and Britain. Many of these incorporated new lighting technologies such as tungsten-halogen bulbs which concealed the necessary transformers within the design. Each country had its own very personal designs and characteristics. Many of the lamps made at the time are still being produced today; others are being reproduced, many in China; others still have become difficult to get hold of but there are many intriguing, efficient and ultimately beautiful lamps available from the 1950s onwards.

Lamps for the mass market

As electric lighting became widespread and taken for granted, so people filled their homes with different forms of lighting; not always to illuminate a desk or area, but sometimes purely for fun. Other lamps, intended to actually illuminate an activity or part of a room, could still present fun images and almost act as little jokes, while supplying the necessary light. In America such lamps were widespread and available in a huge variety of designs.

TV lamps

These lamps were a United States' speciality. In the 1950s when television began to be adopted in most American homes, it also became the focal point in most living rooms. As with any new sort of light source, people feared that watching the flickering bright light in a darkened room could be damaging to the eyes. But early televisions with their dull luminescence were easier to watch in the dark, so enterprising manufacturers began to produce a series of cheap 'TV lamps' which were basically little moulded figurines with a cavity for a light bulb at the back. These would sit proudly on top of the TV providing a low-level illumination so that the contrast between bright screen and dark room was diminished. When the TV was off they acted as amusing small sculptures.

Although not a TV light, this little table lamp with its base of a three-dimensional cockerel and a hen is obviously intended for a living room and is well within the spirit of the idea that lamps should become part of the household as fun objects as well as providing essential light.

TV lamps came in hundreds of designs from many manufacturers. Most of these little lamps were pottery, coated with a shiny colourful glaze, though some were made of plaster. Many were of animals; horses, deer, dogs, birds (a flying mallard was one, for example), cats (such as a group of Siamese cat mother with two kittens), but some had a Japanese influence; others might represent mermaids and a few were abstract. Whether or not they protected TV viewers' eyes, they were tremendously popular and many a television would have more than one sitting on top. Such a lamp had no shade and cast its light onto the wall behind the TV, creating a silhouette of its own shape.

Many of the manufacturers of TV lamps also mass-produced table lamps which were often extraordinarily inventive. Such a lamp might have three bulbs with separate fibreglass or plexiglass shades on a wavy metal stem and you could angle the shades to suit your requirements. Many used fibreglass or plexiglass. These lamps often featured a ceramic figurine which the lamp manufacturers would get various potteries to produce.

Revolving motion lamps

These lamps consisted of a plastic cylinder with a hard plastic top and base. There was an electric bulb inside the lamp and when this warmed up it generated enough heat to create a convection current which caused the thin cut-out stencil cylinder to turn inside the larger glass cylinder. As the pattern of the stencil cylinder passed the bulb it created flickers of light on the paper scene on the outside of the lamp, giving the illusion of a moving picture. Several companies produced these lamps in many different styles from the 1920s to the 1960s, the heyday of their popularity being through the 1920s and 1930s. (Marcel Proust in *À la Recherche du Temps Perdu*, published in 1913, describes a moving lantern placed on top of his bedside table in which a horseman trots out of a hill and 'advances by leaps and bounds towards the castle of Geneviève de Brabant', which must have given a very similar effect.)

Scene-in-Action Corp. of Chicago was one of the first major producers of the revolving motion lamp. There were several popular scenes including a Fountain of Youth, a Forest Fire, and Niagara Falls ('travel to distant places in your own home; see a forest fire rage or the river cascade over Niagara Falls', said one piece of promotional literature). These three original designs were the most popular. When Scene-in-Action ceased production in the 1930s, no more revolving motion lamps were made until Econolite started making them in 1946. They produced at least eleven different models including Mother Goose nursery rhyme scenes, jolly seaside themes and incidents from the lives of famous characters such as Hopalong Cassidy. The company stopped manufacturing lamps in 1961. Most of these lamps are well marked. Scene-in-Action cast their name on the underside of the metal top, while Econolite printed their name and dated each lamp on the shade itself.

Motion picture lamps covered dozens of subjects from Boy Scouts to galloping horses, forest fires, waterfalls or trains and can be of great interest to collectors. They were purely decorative and not meant for 'tasks' such as reading or working. They created a tranquil atmosphere in the room and exceptional patterns on the plastic shade. Many of these lamps used kerosene when they were first introduced but later worked with electric bulbs.

Lava lamps

Just as moving picture lamps were the popular fashion of the 1920s, lava lamps became the craze in the 1950s. The invention of the lava lamp is generally credited to Edward Craven Walker. He worked on his motion lamp, which he called the Astro Light for almost a decade before finally launching it in 1963. His UK-based company Crestworth achieved some success with the lamp but it really took off when the US company Lava Manufacturing Corp. was formed in 1965, founded by two Chicago entrepreneurs, Adolph Wertheimer and Hy Spector. They came across Walker's Astro Light at a trade show in Germany, acquired the US patent rights and began producing a motion lamp of their own.

The ubiquitous lava lamp introduced in the 1950s had a mesmerising effect, although it was useful rather as a moving light sculpture than a serious source of illumination.

Their product, called Lava Lites, is still produced today by Lava World International. Walker's Astro Light also grew in popularity in Europe but sales dropped in the 1980s and Walker sold the Astro Light rights to Mathmos which continues to produce lamps for the market outside the United States, offering modern variations on the basic lamp design.

Twentieth-century designer lights

For the first time the standard central pendant light fittings that were the main source of electric light in most homes were considered to be inadequate as the primary source of light in the home. Modern ideas of lighting increasingly concentrated on providing different types of lighting for different activities or needs and to provide an aesthetically acceptable general light for a room. Individual lamps from the late twentieth century tended to offer more than just one type of light in one fitting. For example, one fitting would often be designed to diffuse the light to provide all-round illumination, while at the same time using an opaque shade to provide an attractive glowing shape.

Designs now began to concentrate on modern materials and techniques such as plastic and aluminium extrusion technology. The development of internal reflector bulbs provided opportunities for plenty of experimentation. Lamps were designed to shine down over a table or to use bulbs with internal reflectors to give upward or downward light. Fittings could be set in different positions to adjust the way the light was directed. The miniaturisation of many lamps and fittings meant that lighting could

Different lighting effects

By this time different types of lighting had acquired their own labels which are useful when discussing the sort of lighting needed in different parts of the home and elsewhere:

General lighting: lights up an area or a space so that you can see your way about and clearly see objects in a room.

Task lighting: task or work lighting is light thrown directly onto a work space, such as a desk, kitchen worktop or a book you are reading so you can see in detail what you are concentrating on.

Uplighters: throw the light beam upwards to reflect off the ceiling, giving a diffused general light for a room or an area of a large room. There are many elegant and

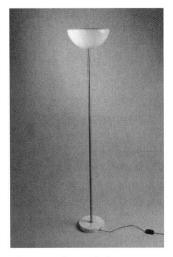

Floor-standing uplighter designed by Achille and Pier Giacomo Castiglioni for Flos has been an influence on many a modern lamp and is practically timeless in its simplicity and elegance. (Photo: Designs of Modernity)

interesting fittings that do this from the Art Deco period and particularly the 1960s onward. Placed carelessly, as they often are, they are inclined to light up cracks in the ceiling or peeling paint, but well-placed, they can give decorative and imaginative warmth to a room. They will only work satisfactorily on a white or very pale surface, which reflects the light back efficiently.

Downlighters: lamps directing light downwards, often fixed to the ceiling or recessed into it, although table lamps with fabric or parchment shades often act both as uplighters and downlighters over a small area. Placed carefully they can give efficient task lighting. Simple chandeliers with five or six bulbs are much more comfortable to live with than a single albeit brighter bulb hanging from the ceiling.

Pendant is a generic term for any lamp hanging from the ceiling, from a bare light bulb to an elaborate chandelier. In the main these provide general lighting rather than lighting for specific tasks, although a rise-and-fall pendant on a pulley system over a table is popular for dining rooms but good too for paperwork when pulled down low over the table.

Pools of light: lamps that create 'pools of light' usually serve no particular purpose other than to make a room more interesting, softer and friendlier, although occasionally the light may be at a high enough level to read by. Many antique lamps are excellent at creating such light, from the highly decorative paraffin/kerosene parlour lamps that were such a feature in nineteenth-century America to the fairy and tea lights that gave a gentle glow in a living room or bedroom to the wondrous opalescent shades of Tiffany and his followers whose main purpose was to beautify a room with light.

Accent lighting is used to bring life to a picture, plant or sculpture. Many picture lights are available, usually in brass – good when fixed to the object they are lighting or near to it, so that the beam doesn't have to cross the room and glare in people's eyes.

be placed in many places in the domestic interior and lamps themselves could be miniature *objets d'art*.

In the 1950s, 60s and 70s lighting became much more architectural. By the 1960s lighting techniques were providing a scheme of several fittings for domestic interiors. Manufacturing companies often commissioned prominent architects and designers to produce their lighting designs, frequently using brushed aluminium for the shade which might have a lacquer on the outside, designed to minimise any reflected glare. Companies in Scandinavia and Italy in particular became well-known for the lamps they produced. The emphasis was on elegance and geometric shapes, thin metal stands and metal shades. Table lamps used fabric or plastic shades with large flamboyant and colourful designs in stylised floral patterns.

The development of interior reflector bulbs provided possibilities for experimentation in lighting techniques, and a transformer and an appropriate current change make it possible to use low-voltage directional lamps for reading and the spotlighting of a sculpture or surface for special effects. Used in conjunction with floor or table lamps of a more diffusing character, these fittings blended a diffused and soft-shadowed light with the more local directional lighting so suitable for domestic surroundings. Pendant fittings could be both directional and diffusing, although each type would be used in different circumstances. Many successful twentieth-century designer lamps are still in production or being reproduced today.

The architect designers

Many architects turned their hand to designing both furniture and lighting. Early in the century people like Poul Henningsen (1894–1967) in Denmark had found the style of traditional lighting insufficient for their interiors and had begun designing their own solutions. Henningsen was evangelistic on the subject of modern lighting and depressed by 'how dismal people's homes are'. He realised that electric light gave the possibility

This is Jill, a low-voltage uplighter of great elegance and style giving enough reflected light to illuminate a small room. The glass shade is acid-etched and sandblasted and the built-in dimmer switch gives the lamp great flexibility. It was designed by Perry King, Santiago Miranda and G.L. Arnaldi for Flos in 1978.

Geometric designs such as this cone-shaped fabric lampshade were popular during the 1950s. This table light has a carved wheel-shaped base – also a popular design.

Some characteristics of later twentieth-century lamps

- Counterweights were used to create pivoting arms. One of the best-known of these was the Tizio lamp but there were many others designed on the same principle, including the Samurai task light from Stilnovo and a number of low-voltage tungsten-halogen lights in which the counterweight was housed in the transformer. In fact, individual low-voltage lamps showed some very creative ways of incorporating the transformer into the design of the lamp itself.
- Discs: horizontal circular flat 'plates' often used as diffusers or as reflector surfaces to bounce the light off or they might be both diffusers and reflectors at the same time. They were elegant and often used, as so many pendants were, over a dining or work table.
- Hemispheres with their generous bowl shapes were popular as floor lamps, pendants, table and wall fittings. The light source concealed inside the opaque or diffusing bowl provided a friendly area of glowing light.
- Right angles became popular and were often used for uplighters, wall and table lights. The angles were softened by having rounded corners.
- Adjustable angled lamps were popular for desks, often on a counterweight, often angled in several different directions, sometimes flexible like a snake.
- Swivelling shades were used for desk and bedside lights and there were a number of little lamps in which you could more or less turn the light off by swivelling the shade over the bulb.
- Bare bulbs were sometimes used, particularly in the 1960s, to show off the light source, though by this time, the bulbs themselves were much more diverse with low-voltage bulbs which gave particularly sparkly light in themselves and silvered bulbs that could diffuse and direct the light. By now there was an enormous choice of bulbs, each producing a different effect. To avoid glare it is best to use low-voltage or crown silvered bulbs in this sort of lamp.
- Mesh panels were sometimes used to conceal the light source. They were inspired by commercial lighting (the hi-tech look) which created a mysterious, spangled effect.
- Cone shapes were often used for lampshades and bases, the shape echoing a widening beam of light spreading out from the bulb.

of 'wallowing in light'. His two most successful lamps designed for Poulson were the PH lamp in 1924 and the Artichoke lamp (1958), both of which have become influences on modern design. Like his contemporaries he was aware of the differences in tones between levels of intensity and tried to create the most balanced effect. He varied internal colours of shades to give off light from different parts of the spectrum to contribute to the overall interior environment.

Many designers were intrigued by the possibilities of creating light and many of them made their mark by producing innovative and influential lamp and lighting designs. These include Poul Henningsen, Piet Hein, Arne Jacobsen and Tore Ahlsén from Scandinavia; Gino Sarfatti, Fabio Lenci, Renzo Piano, Afra and Tobia Scarpa, and Achille and Pier Giacomo Castiglioni and many others from Italy; Verner Panton from Switzerland and Richard Sapper from the USA. Many of the most important manufacturers of light fittings were small-scale companies with restricted output, often producing innovative experimental fittings, very like works of art, that larger companies would be unlikely to risk.

This pendant lamp, the PH Artichoke was designed by the Danish designer Poul Henningsen in 1958 and produced by Louis Poulsen. It has been in production ever since and has acquired iconic status.

The Italians turned to completely new ideas for lighting. Their lamps became more and more inventive and decorative, providing different types of light for different areas in the home. Scandinavia's long dark winters and early nights led to a preference for light colours, reflective surfaces, minimal clutter, the use of light-coloured unfinished woods such as beech, birch, white pine and alder with whitewashed surfaces or stained with pale blues, and equivalently bright lighting. Where the Italians turned to minimalist designs and modern metals, the Scandinavians used paper and wood or metal with wing-like panels and concentrated largely on pendant ceiling lights. The Danish architect Carl Thore, designing in the 1960s and 1970s created a series of multilayered modern ceiling lights.

So it can be seen that twentieth-century designers and artists were fascinated by the challenge of turning his/her hand to designing the perfect lamp and many small, often family manufacturers sprang up to turn these designs into reality.

Some twentieth-century lighting milestones

The following are lamps created between the 1920s and the 1970s which were highly innovative and greatly influenced the design of lamps that came after them. Many of them are still in production or are being reproduced.

The PH Lamp (1924)

<u>Scandinavian</u>: this was a multi-shaded lamp designed by Poul Henningsen and produced by Louis Poulsen. It was also called the Paris lamp because it won an award at the Paris World Exhibition. It incorporated tiers of small shades, allowing the user to divert light in several directions without exposing the light source. This lamp is still produced today and has an undeniable 'presence' and grace.

Best Lite (1930)

<u>British</u>: designed by Robert Dudley Best and produced by Best & Lloyd. Its initial reception was lukewarm and it started existence mainly in car repair shops where it provided a superbly functional light. It was only when it was described by the *Architects' Journal* in Britain as 'the first Bauhaus manifestation in the UK' that architects began to sit up and take notice. Winston Churchill had one installed on his desk in the government bunker under Whitehall during World War Two and that was when the lamp began to have a popular success. The Best Lite is a masterpiece of classic simplicity still in production today.

The Best Lite was designed in 1930 by Robert Dudley Best and produced by his company Best & Lloyd. This one has been cleaned up and rewired. You can see the ultra simple angling device on the stem. (Seen at Turn On)

Anglepoise (1934)

<u>British</u>: designed by George Carwardine, an automotive engineer who owned a factory in Bath which developed vehicle suspension systems. The first model remained in continuous production for over thirty years; refinements were made but the Anglepoise is still produced with little change. There were many copies of the Anglepoise. Its unadorned practicality and efficiency appealed to architects and then percolated through to the general public. One particular lamp that showed its influence was a counterbalanced lamp by a British company, Hadrill & Horstmann. The lamp, which appeared in the late 1940s, was a desk lamp (looking not unlike the Anglepoise) which took a maximum 25-watt bulb.

The early Anglepoise lamp remained in production for over thirty years and is being produced today with only a few amendments. (Photo: Morris Interiors)

A short history of the Anglepoise lamp

Cawardine loved to tinker in his workshop and especially enjoyed developing different types of springs. During these experiments, he designed a new type of spring which could be moved easily in every direction yet could also remain rigid when held in position. He patented his spring design in 1932 and eventually found a suitable use for it – a lamp which, supported and balanced by a sequence of springs, could be constantly repositioned to focus the light in specific directions. The lamp could be both flexible and stable, like a human arm. He designed a heavy base for stability and a shade which could concentrate the beam on specific points without causing dazzle. This focused beam enabled the lamp to consume less electricity than existing models. Carwardine intended it at first for the workmen in his factory to illuminate particular components but he soon realised that it would be equally suitable for illuminating the papers and books in homes and offices.

Carwardine licensed his lamp to Herbert Terry & Sons, a manufacturer based at Redditch in Worcestershire which was already supplying springs to his factory. It was patented as Anglepoise. The first version of the Anglepoise lamp, the 1208, was produced by Terry in 1934 with four springs. It proved so popular that two years later Terry introduced a domestic version, the 1227 with three springs and an Art Deco-inspired three-tier base, which looked more stylish than the single-tier base of the 1208. One of the benefits of the 1227 is that it worked perfectly with an inexpensive 25-watt bulb which, Terry's advertising claimed, was as efficient in the Anglepoise lamp as a 60-watt bulb would be in another light.

Three years later Terry introduced a new version of the 1227, with a two-tier base and a wider shade which was capable of taking a 40-watt bulb. This model remained in production for over thirty years and is still widely regarded as the archetypal Anglepoise, even though the design has since been modified.

Le Klint (1943)

Scandinavian: classic folded and pleated paper shades, still in production today. Strands of metal, wood and glass were added over the years and the design has become a classic. Both shades and stands are still being folded by hand.

Bubble Lamp (1947)

American: designed by architect and designer George Nelson (1908–86) and produced by Howard Miller. The Bubble Lamp was made of steel with a special translucent white plastic shade which could be used with any coloured bulb. It was an extremely simple idea and gave an effect not unlike the ephemeral Chinese paper shades that became so ubiquitous in the 1980s and 90s. The lamp could be supported on wrought iron legs or suspended from the ceiling and could be raised and lowered by a counterweight system. There were several variations of shade; saucer-shaped, bowl-shaped, elongated shape and so on. Nelson never named the different lamp designs in the series. They were simply given numbers, so a large ball lamp was sold under 'Bubble Lamp H725' and a large saucer lamp 'Bubble Lamp H727'.

Luminator (1955)

Italian: minimalist light designed by Achille Castiglioni and manufactured by Flos. The Castiglioni Brothers, Achille and Pier Giacomo set up a design office in 1944 and became one of the wittiest and most elegant and innovative partnerships in modern design. An astonishing number of timeless lamp designs was one

This is an early floor-standing Anglepoise, still in its original state. Such lamps are hard to find nowadays but the original version is still being produced.

result of this partnership. Other famous lamps by Achille Castiglioni include the Bulb (1957), the Arco (*qv*), and the Snoopy lamp (1967), inspired by the muzzle of the cartoon character.

Gino Chandelier (1958)

Italian: designed by Gino Sarfatti (1912–84), an aeronaval engineer. From 1939 he worked on lighting design and set up the company Arteluce which soon became a national and international influence on modern architectural lighting design. Gino Sarfatti designed and produced more than 400 luminaires and carried out research into innovation in materials, production technologies, light sources, technical lighting effects and design aspects.

A J table lamp (1958)

Scandinavian: designed by Arne Jacobsen for Louis Poulsen, an elegant lamp designed for the SAS Royal Hotel in Copenhagen. It has a distinct asymmetrical shape with tiltable head, specifically for reading. The cut-out hollow at the base was originally intended to hold an ash-tray but can now be considered part of the sculptural quality of the design.

Taccia table lamp (1962)

Italian: designed by the Castiglioni brothers for Flos; a generous open bowl facing upwards on a stubby base, providing direct and reflected light.

Kvadrille (1960s)

Scandinavian: designed by Bent Karlby using coloured metal sheets, for Lyfa.

Arco floor lamp (1962)

Italian: designed by Achille and Pier Giacomo Castiglioni and produced by Flos. This splendid lamp had a base of marble and an enormous long curved arm 8ft (2.5m) from the base with the shade pointing downwards. The lamp was designed to be moved by inserting a broomstick through the hole in the base.

The Arco lamp designed by Achille and Pier Giacomo Castiglioni has been the inspiration for several large arched floor lamps. Its marble base keeps it stable and has a hole designed to take a broomstick in case the lamp needs to be moved.

Cantilever desk light (1966)

British: Designed by Gerald Abramowitz for Best & Lloyd. In 1966 the company received the Design Centre Award for this remarkably forward-looking (even for the 1960s) minimalist lamp.

Symfoni (1967)

Scandinavian: designed by Claus Bolby. Bolby was born in 1944 and began his career as a technician in the Royal Danish Air Force. He designed an acrylic pendant light in his own workshop for a new church. He then created a smaller version of the same acrylic light for private homes, which he called Symfoni, and started producing it in the basement of his home, selling through retail shops. In the 1960s, he performed all kinds of chemical experiments in his cellar with acrylic pieces left over from Symfoni production and also introduced bubbles into the acrylic which acted like prisms, producing a warm glow which became very popular particularly in Denmark.

An arched lamp very similar to the Arco, but perhaps less grandiose; this one has an interesting mechanism for altering its direction and a metal rather than a marble base.

Eclisse table lamp (1967)

Italian: designed by Vico Magestretti for Artemide. Fat little rounded base and rotatable bulb shield in white lacquered steel with ability to cut the light source and regulate light emission.

Periscopio (1968)
Italian: an enamelled steel desk lamp that looked a bit like a periscope, by Danilo and Corrado Aroldi for Stilnovo.

Tizio desk lamp (1972)
Italian: an elegant cantilevered lamp designed by the US designer Richard Sapper, produced by Artemide. The position and the direction of the bulb could be easily adjusted thanks to two counterweights. Two other features of the lamp were the lack of wires, (the two parallel arms were used to conduct electricity to the bulb) and the halogen bulb, which was previously mainly used in the automotive industry.

The Tizio desk lamp was designed in 1972 by Richard Sapper for Artemide. It is beautifully cantilevered and weighted heavily at the base.

Cubo table lamp (1970s)
Italian: designed by Franco Bettonica and Mario Melocchi at Studio Opi and produced by Cinie Nils of Italy. The red plastic cube (4 x 4 x 4.25in; 10 x 10 x 11cm) was designed to sit on a table and was turned on and off by raising or lowering the lid. The design is back in production today but the originals can still sometimes be found (which may or may not conform to modern safety regulations). (See picture on p. 85.)

Gibigiana (1980)
Italian: a tiny reflector light with polished mirror surface for bedside reading, designed by Achille Castiglioni for Flos.

Taraxacum (1988)
Italian: designed by Achille Castiglioni for Flos; a pendant lamp designed to look like a dandelion head with many bulbs screwed into a central stem.

An angled desk lamp in black metal, using low-voltage lighting with an integral dimmer switch.

Things you should know when buying twentieth-century lamps

If you are buying a lamp because you love it and want to use it in your home, you can make your own decisions about its condition. But if you are a serious collector, there are things you should look out for:

- Check that the light really is what the seller claims it is. A few unscrupulous sellers do deliberately set out to mislead but most false attributions come from sellers who simply repeat unsubstantiated information from other sources.
- Sometimes an incorrect designer or manufacturer is attributed to a genuinely collectible light. Sometimes a copy of a valuable original is offered as the original. Many modern light designs from the 1960s and 70s for example were widely copied for a market eager to adopt but unable to afford the innovative but expensive productions and it's not unusual today for poorer quality look-alikes and imitations to be attributed to the wrong companies.
- Check the light's condition carefully and if buying online ask the seller for a condition report if none is provided. The resale value of a vintage light drops significantly if there are scratches, rust, dents, bends and other damage but some sellers do not take this into account when setting their own prices.
- Beware of terms like 'patina' being used as a euphemism for damage. Patination is a natural outcome of age and normal use in materials like wood and copper and is not the result of injury or exposure to poor conditions.
- Beware of vague phrases such as 'As you would expect in a lamp this age'. Many lamps from the 1960s and 70s are in near perfect condition.
- Look out for interventions such as repainting, which will destroy the value of all but the most exceptionally rare vintage lamps and significantly reduce even those.
- Check that there are no missing parts. Some lights such as Verner Panton's Flowerpot for Louis Poulsen and Jo Hammerborg's Saturn and E. Balslev's Radius for Fog & Mörup have parts that have to be removed to replace the bulb. It's quite common for these to go missing altogether, so check before you buy.
- Don't assume that lighting from the twentieth century is safe or legal. The electric components and the wiring of many vintage lights are often in poor condition so make sure such lights are dismantled and checked. And remember that different countries still have different laws. For example, legislation in the UK requires that metal-bodied lighting should have a three-core wiring and bulb-holder but

vintage Danish lighting nearly always comes with a two-core set-up. However, if you are a serious collector, remember that removing or altering the original components may have a small impact on the light's value.

- Check that the light is, indeed, a vintage original and not a later production or reissue. Many vintage designs are still in production or back in production by the original or a different manufacturer. These, even if identical, will not increase in value in the same way as an original vintage example. (Copies are made on the cheap, many in China. They may look almost identical, but the materials and components may not be the same as the originals.)

Light bulbs for vintage lamps

Whatever electric lamp you buy, whatever age it is, the light bulb you use in it can be important. Older filament bulbs are the nearest to what would have been used in older lamps and will give the nearest to the quality of light they would originally have produced. But newer bulbs can give subtler light or more directed light or more economical light and provided the lamp has been wired to modern safety standards and the bulbs have the same basic fittings, you can choose what bulbs you like.

Some types of bulb suitable for use with vintage lighting:

- Filament light bulbs: still the most commonly used type of bulb used for general lighting and task lighting.
- Compact fluorescent (CFLs): energy-efficient bulbs with long lives which come in a variety of shapes, and can be used for both general and task lighting. They will last for much longer than filament bulbs and can achieve significant savings in costs of energy and replacement bulbs.
- Tungsten-halogen bulbs (TH lamps): used in some later twentieth-century downlighters, uplighters and wall-washer fittings. This is a form of filament lamp in which the coiled filament is mounted in a narrow tubular envelope of fused silica. The gas filling of the envelope contains a halogen gas which has the property of combining with tungsten in certain conditions. When the tungsten molecules 'boil off' the filament, they are captured by the halogen molecules. The halogen molecules have an affinity for tungsten and are attracted back to the filament and so help to prevent it thinning. But at filament temperature, the

tungsten-halogen molecules break up and the halogen returns to the gas filling to await the capture of another tungsten molecule – thus completing the 'halogen cycle'. Because a tungsten-halogen lamp operates at a higher temperature than other filament lamps, the lamp is more efficient and produces whiter light.

- Reflector bulbs (mushroom bulbs): filament bulbs with an internally silvered reflector, used for indoor highlighting and effect lighting. PAR (parabolic aluminised reflector) bulbs are similar to reflector bulbs except they are housed in a robust pressed glass envelope and can be used for garden lighting. Both types have screw fittings.
- Reproductions of antique bulbs are available which may be considered more suitable for antique lamps than modern bulbs.
- Not all antique lamps can cope with a high-wattage bulb. If in doubt, use a low-wattage bulb so as not to damage the lamp and also to get the most genuine original effect.

These bubble lamps were produced in the 1960s and 1970s by E.S. Horn Belysning of Denmark. They had self-coloured wiring and their robust ball-shaped metal heads were held in place by a magnet in the base and can be freely swivelled round. (www.classic-modern. co.uk)

Holophane glass was invented to diffuse the light and make it less glaring. This classic pendant has influenced the design of many later pendant shades and Holophane glass has been used for many factory lights. (Photo: Antique Lighting Company)

The Swedish designer Poul Henningsen designed this lamp in the 1930s and it has remained popular and in production since then with very good reason. It is good-looking, of great simplicity though not severe, and the shade can be lacquered in different colours. (Photo: Designs of Modernity)

This attractive red metal factory pendant lamp takes some of its inspiration from the PH lamp. It has a caged bulb for safety and comes from Eastern Europe. (Photo: Trainspotters)

Industrial and public lighting

Among the most interesting types of lighting for collectors is nineteenth- and twentieth-century industrial lighting. There is lighting from factories and from hospitals, lighting from large offices and laboratories. Then there is lighting from cruise liners, first-class railway carriages and hotels. Much of this lighting incorporates modern thinking on being functional, simple and efficient.

Unlikely though it may seem, medical lighting can range from decorative Victorian pieces to futuristic dentist's lamps. What once shone a piercing light onto an operating table can now be a bold statement hanging over a conference or dining table. Early electrified examples of operating lights had japanned finishes (copper-washed brass with black stripes, say) with milk or emerald glass shades. Bright sleek metal lights from the 1930s to 50s are sanitary and hygienic. Designs of that period could be found in aluminium, stainless steel and chrome and are very sympathetic to twenty-first-century furnishings.

The next generation of vintage lights?

From the introduction of electricity in the late nineteenth century, there has been a constant search for longer-lasting, cheaper, and more convenient versions of the basic light source.

LEDs

The latest technological advance in lighting is the LED or light emitting diode. LEDs do many different jobs and are found in all kinds of devices. Among other things they form the numbers on digital clocks, transmit information from remote controls and tell you when your appliances are turned on. Basically LEDs are tiny light bulbs that fit easily into an electrical circuit. Unlike ordinary incandescent bulbs they don't have a filament that will burn out and they don't get very hot. They are illuminated solely by the movement of electrons in a semiconductor material and they last just as long as a standard transistor. A diode is the simplest possible semiconductor device and is therefore an excellent beginning point for understanding how semiconductors work. This electron energy is converted to light as electrons flow through the device.

LED lighting is still in its infancy as far as home lighting is concerned. Domestic lighting usually calls for the use of white light but LEDs can only produce a specific colour of the spectrum. So how can LED technology be used to produce the white light needed for lighting the home? There are various possibilities. The first, discovered in Japan in 1996, is to coat a blue LED with white phosphor. When blue light hits the inner surface of the phosphor, it emits white light. This technology is now seen in commercial applications but there are still some worries about the life-cycle of the technology. Phosphor can degrade over a period of years, reducing the light output. The second method is to mix the three colours, red, green and blue, although the white light thus created tends not to be very even in its spectrum.

Research continues and in the meantime LED lights are already available for reading and other lamps in the home and they do have several benefits. They are long-lived, they provide the kind of light that will produce highlights on silver and glass, and they are already exceeding the energy efficiency of tungsten-filament and tungsten-halogen lamps. They offer significant energy and carbon savings in the long term. Most (though not all) are much more energy efficient than incandescent light sources and a switch-over to 100 per cent LED lighting in the home would produce enormous savings in electricity bills.

Much money and creative thinking is being concentrated on the development of the technology at present; we will have to wait to see how their aesthetic design develops and wait for the creative designs to catch up with the creative technology.

In the home LEDs are likely to make their first main impact in task lighting, table and desk lamps, under-cupboard kitchen lighting and accent lighting. For LEDs to make a major impact in the home a complete change is required in how we view home lighting. LEDs could be fitted into architectural mouldings or window frames and sills. They offer the chance to design curved and other three-dimensional lighting surfaces and to place the light sources in the orientation required. They are sheet materials that could be used for 'wallpaper' or self-luminous lamp 'shades'.

Some LED lighting facts

- Low power consumption compared with conventional lighting.
- No ultra-violet output (the UV component of conventional lighting can cause damage to fabric).
- Very little heat is produced in the light output, reducing the cost of building air-conditioning and allowing lighting to fit into positions too small for conventional lights.
- The life of the lamps is estimated at 100,000 hours.
- Ecologically friendly.
- Lightweight to manufacture and to install.
- Coloured light can be produced by controlling the power to each primary colour.
- The light can be uncomfortably bright.
- The technology requires completely new thinking and so far LED lights for the home are few and far between.

So far the first LEDs still have a few drawbacks: they can produce a lot of heat at the 'chip' level that must be conducted away to avoid shortening of the LED lifetime; they also create an uncomfortably bright light (a reflection of the first introduction of electric light!).

CHAPTER FOUR

Materials and Manufacturers

In the search for satisfactory light, many fuels have been tried and many materials and techniques have been used to contain the fuel and to support and enhance the light source. Some have been particularly effective. Materials used for protecting the flame or diffusing the light include metal, rock crystal, glass, stone, wood, paper, parchment and plastic. From a bashed-out piece of tin for a child's 'chamberstick' to the elegant neo-classical candelabra of the eighteenth century and the exotic and erotic figures in spelter and other metals of the Art Nouveau and Art Deco periods, materials used for lighting have been many and wonderful. Stones such as alabaster and marble, early plastics such as Bakelite (particularly for plugs and switches) have all had their place in lighting.

There is no dearth of antique and vintage lamps to be discovered, from the earliest and most primitive tin and brass to the most glittering seventeenth- and eighteenth-century chandeliers through the many historical styles the Victorians liked so much to mid twentieth-century modernist and industrial lighting. Between the 1840s and early 1900s oil lamps and candelabra co-existed with early electric lamps, so there is a wealth of different styles of lamp available to complement traditional architecture or decorate the modern home.

Many early candle-holders were made of wood, in the days when forests were many and wood easy to get hold of. The earliest medieval pendant candle-holders were often made of wooden crosses with a candle fixed at the end of each arm. Metal has been a mainstay in the manufacture of candle-holders and lanterns, lamp bases, reflectors and light-bulb holders, anything from tin, iron, brass, bronze, pewter and silver. Glass became important as the material for chimneys when oil and paraffin became common.

This is an eighteenth-century Welsh candle and rushlight-holder with a turned fruitwood base, pitted with age, but the more attractive for it. It is surrounded by typical furniture of its time including bentwood chairs and a fine oak table. (Photo: Country Oak Antiques)

In this chapter we look at some of the important materials used in vintage lights and some of the manufacturers and designers responsible for producing them. Many were based in Europe, others operated in the United States. Although some of the best-known and most influential manufacturers and designers are listed here, it is only the most dedicated collector or *aficionado* who will want to buy the now very expensive items created by them. But imitation is the purest form of flattery and there were many artists and designers in every age who produced similar lamps to the famous ones, and many interesting and beautiful lamps that reflect their period with elegance and truth that may be equally desirable and much more affordable. So by all means get to recognise and know the originals but don't imagine they are the only items worth owning. There are plenty of wonderful designs out there simply waiting for a good home.

An imposing eighteenth-century floor-standing oak candlestick; its height can be adjusted by screwing the branch section round the thread on the stand. (Photo: Country Oak Antiques)

Candle-holders made of wood

In countries rich in woods and forests, wood has been an invaluable resource for candlesticks and rushlight-holders, for table and floor lamps with barley twist stems and for very early pendant candle-holders. Wood used for candlesticks in England, for example, included oak, pine and fruit woods.

Antique examples of wooden items are still around, although no longer very easy to find. Each piece was hand-carved and therefore unique and by now wooden pieces have achieved a patina with age, with a strength, finish and individuality that gives them enormous charm.

During the early twentieth century Scandinavian designers in particular (their country being largely covered in forests) often used slender wood shavings for shades for their modern lamps, which complemented the characteristic Scandinavian wooden furniture that became so popular during the 1950s and 60s, noted for its modern elegance while using traditional techniques and materials. Wooden bases both primitive and exotic, plain, varnished or painted have always been used for lamp bases.

'Celebrity' makers versus the less well-known

For the serious collector of antique and vintage lights, details are important, such as designers, manufacturers, types of material used and so on. There are many people involved in the evolution and designs of lamps throughout the ages who have become important because of their own wonderful inventions and designs and because of the influence they had on other makers. If you are a beginner and interested in finding out more, then these names are important too and will give you a better understanding of the whole subject or the particular period in which you are interested.

The wooden base of this interesting table lamp is brightly painted and the shade is of spatter glass. Probably early twentieth-century, it has an oriental and timeless look about it.

It is useful to remember that many lamps were made by manufacturers whose names have been rather eclipsed by the celebrity 'name' lamps, but that many of them had just as much merit as the better-known lamp designers and manufacturers; there are many worthwhile lamps that have no name, no stamp of authenticity but which are well-made, beautiful and efficient. So if you are not set on a particular lamp, designer or manufacturer, simply go for ones you like.

Tiffany lamps provide a good example. During his time his lamps became so well-known that the Tiffany name has become the generic term for the highly-decorated glass lampshades his studio produced, but in America at the same time a number of manufacturers were producing lamps very similar to his. Although a Tiffany lamp nowadays can cost a fortune, lamps made by other manufacturers of the time are still to be found and can be excellent bargains.

The same is true of many of the lamps produced in the second half of the twentieth century. There are many famous names both of designers and manufacturers, but lamps were being produced at the same time following the same ideas which can be equally attractive and quite a lot cheaper. Of course, as a collector, you will be entranced by a lamp that can be traced back to one of the famous lighting designers such as Gino Sarfatti, Poul Henningsen or Ingo Maurer but as a homemaker, you might enjoy just as much a similar lamp by an unknown

This sturdy little metal kerosene lantern from the USA would have been used on the railroads around the turn of the twentieth century.

Work lanterns

- Lighting devices of many kinds were used on the railways including lanterns and lamps, distinguished by their construction which was designed to protect the interior light source. Early railway workers relied on lanterns for relaying signals and inspecting trains at night. They burned paraffin/kerosene, signal oil or other types of fuel. Each was designed for a specific job: some were used by workers on the line, others by inspectors and others again by conductors. In the USA any lantern that carries a railway marking is valued by collectors. Many types of lamps and lanterns were used in railway systems including marker lamps which were hung on rolling stock to indicate the rear of the train.
- There were also miners' lamps, ships' lamps, each with its own particular function and therefore its shape, size and colour. Depending on their function lamps could have a single lens or multiple lenses and some lamps had lenses of different colours. Although combustible-fuel lanterns were gradually phased out, they were made of stern stuff and many have survived and constitute a special category for collecting and restoration.
- In the early 1950s propane fuel in small portable cylinders led to the development of propane lanterns as an alternative to paraffin-fuelled lanterns.

designer, or even an unabashed simple 'fun' lamp such as a shining plastic pineapple with the bulb inside.

Some metals used for lamps

Iron

Few iron lamp bases are left for collectors. But in the beginning much iron was used, made by local blacksmiths for sturdy floor-standing candle-holders, rush-lamp holders, and primitive candle sconces. If lamps were made of iron rather than brass, they were often called 'stable' candlesticks

These iron candlesticks and rushlight-holders all originated in Ireland where iron implements of this kind were generally more solid and robust than those made in England. (Photo: Country Oak Antiques)

– suitable only for use in stables and out of doors; if made of brass they would be intended for indoor use.

Brass

Brass is an alloy predominantly of copper with the addition of zinc and sometimes lead or tin. Very old brass may have as much as 12 per cent tin but Regency and Victorian brass had only 1 per cent. Crock-brass was a term used for the copper lead alloy which was used mainly for casting domestic pots. It has a muted yellow colour, similar to gold and doesn't tarnish easily. Early on in lighting history, polished brass was used as mirrored sconces to reflect the light of wall-hung candles behind the candle-holder, which helped to intensify the light.

This sort of iron 'cage' candle-holder would have been made for use in a stable or outbuilding and was often called a stable candlestick. (Photo: Country Oak Antiques)

Large profits were to be made from brass. Numerous foundries and factories grew like mushrooms from the late eighteenth century on, and by the time Queen Victoria came to the throne in 1837 Birmingham was the centre of brass industry in Britain. Brass-making was broken down into nine types: casting, cabinet, bell and general brass foundry; naval; crock-making; plumber's brass foundry; stamped work; rolled brass wire and sheathing; tube manufacture; lamp-making; gas and electric fittings. Originally the alloy was imported from Bristol and the goods finished in Birmingham.

The first Birmingham brass works was Turner's Brass, set up in 1740. Brass fittings were in demand for many things and in particular for steam engines. By the end of the century Birmingham was also producing brass fittings for gas lamps and there were seventy-one brass founders in the city. Brass was used for oil lamp burners, the burner being the part that held the fuel and the point of combustion. It evolved over many centuries but the design basically remained the same: a piece of brass moulded into some form to hold a wick and a chimney which protected the flame from the air and aided combustion by creating

The brass base of this handsome English paraffin/kerosene lamp with its blue glass reservoir badly needs a bit of care and attention but will look good when polished up. (Seen in Paul's Emporium)

This proudly polished little North American kerosene lamp was designed to be fixed to a wall, but it projects far enough out from the wall not to singe it. Here you can see the burner, which would have been covered by a glass chimney when in use.

a draught. Most lamp manufacturers made the metal parts and bought the glass from other companies.

Bronze

An alloy predominantly of copper with additions of tin and sometimes lead and zinc in varying proportions. Over the centuries these proportions often changed, but bronze always contains tin. Bronze alloys expand slightly just before they set, so they will fill in the finest details of a mould. This made bronze popular for Art Nouveau and Art Deco sculptural figures, often naked women, designed to hold the light source.

Silver

Georgian Silver Candlesticks

Many eighteenth-century English candlesticks were cast in vase-like shapes and then worked on with special tools to bring out the design by hammering, chiselling, embossing, engraving and other ways of working the surface of the silver. They might be designed with flowers, acanthus leaves and the popular shell of the French rococo style. This was known as the High Standard style which began in 1696. Between 1696 and 1720 silver was made of an alloy higher than sterling (then spelled stirling) in order to discourage the practice of melting down coins for objects of domestic use. As it was softer than sterling, objects had to be simpler so that the baluster form as used in Queen Anne's time is quite severe and unornamented.

After the return to the standard of sterling, more ornamental forms could be made. At this time there was a general tendency towards all things French and in silver specifically there was the influence of the presence of the French Huguenot silversmiths who had come in great numbers to England to escape persecution.

English silver after 1720 began to be very elaborate and to show many graceful forms derived from the French love of floral forms, curves and an elaborate style generally. The square bases of the seventeenth century began to be eight-sided, rounded or scalloped and some of these were very elaborate with a conventionalised shell ornament. The vase-shaped stem began to disappear and the Greek column, generally fluted and headed by a Corinthian capital, was fashionable. The foot became square but unlike the seventeenth-century foot it was high and the sloping, concave sides offered additional space for classic ornament of perhaps a lion's head. Laurel wreaths, acanthus leaves and paterae or rosette-shaped ornaments were other Greek or classic motifs favoured by the silversmiths.

Silver candelabra with several branches were popular for dining table decoration, on sideboards and mantelpieces up to the early twentieth century (while there were still servants to do the cleaning and polishing).

A contorted gilt rococo candlestick, possibly French, showing how candlesticks into the late eighteenth and early nineteenth centuries became more and more ornate with lavish foliage and scrolls.

Throughout the entire Georgian period, which extended through the first quarter of the nineteenth century, Greek influence was felt in successive waves.

By the 1730s Georgian silver candlesticks had become taller with a richer ornamentation. In the 1740s candlesticks had removable sconces or nozzles. The silver of this period is very charming. Skilled workmanship continued through the nineteenth century and much Victorian silver is highly desirable.

During the Regency period from 1790 to 1820, candlesticks became increasingly ornate with lavish foliage and scrolls to the base, around the top of the stem and around the socket. The rococo style became popular and ornate candlesticks were produced. The rounded base became popular too. Cast silver candlesticks are very few from this period because it was so expensive to produce them. The new mechanised method of making candlesticks was cheaper and more practical.

Three out of the many silversmiths perhaps worth mentioning who produced candlesticks are **Paul de Lamerie** (1688–1751), the best-known English silversmith of his generation who produced a great deal of work from the 1730s and was appointed goldsmith to George I in 1716. He produced many fine examples of rococo Georgian silver candlesticks for the rich. Centuries later, around 1900 **Archibald Knox** was commissioned by Liberty of London to design pieces for Liberty's 'Cymric' silverware and Tudric pewter ware range based on Celtic designs, and is known to have produced around 400 designs. Among them were several silver candelabra and candlesticks. **Arthur Silver** was another designer commissioned by Liberty to design for the 'Cymric' range and, like Knox, he designed candlesticks among other silver items. It is difficult to attribute particular designs to any artist who worked for Liberty as the designers were not acknowledged publicly.

This eighteenth-century metal wall bracket for a candle is both inventive and decorative, carefully designed to keep the flame at a distance from the wall. (Photo: Country Oak Antiques)

Tin

Tin was used for the most basic of lamps and was probably hammered into various candle-holding shapes by a local tinsmith. Tin was used for primitive candle wall sconces, hurricane lamps and other household candle-holders.

Other metals

Twentieth-century designers have used many materials including aluminium, stainless steel and chrome for lamp shades and bases. These might be lacquered in bright colours or left in their pristine metal state.

Some metal lamp manufacturers

By the 1920s the standard design for a table lamp was a bowl-shaped reservoir, pressurised by air from either a built-in or a separate pump, a fuel riser, a valve, a generator to vaporise the fuel and a burner above one or two inverted mantles. All the major manufacturers produced something along these lines including Tilley, Coleman, AGM, Evening Star, Petromax and Primus and the lamps produced by all of them were very similar.

Various metals were used for lamps. The metal gave a shiny reflection which enhanced the light and would have been something to show off to guests. This ceiling lamp has a small smoke bell which can just be seen above the chimney.

Below are just some of the lamp manufacturers who produced pieces that can still be found in second-hand shops, antique shops and flea markets today.

Britain

W.A.S. Benson, London, c.1880–1920: designed and set up his own workshop to make art metalware including tableware and oil, gas and electric light fittings, which were retailed through Morris & Company. Eventually these were mass-produced and sold through Liberty of London. He was closely associated with William Morris and the Arts and Crafts movement.

Bullpitt & Sons, Birmingham: originally brass founders, later specialised in lamps and copper kettles (eventually registered Swan brand, famous for their kettles).

Curtiss & Harvey, Wandsworth, London: from around 1919 to the 1930s. Curtiss & Harvey made the Evening Star lamp which acted both as a table lamp and a hurricane lantern and was described as 'giving a wonderful light of 300 cp from paraffin or petrol, easy to light and operate'. The lamps were supplied with a separate external pump, similar to the American Coleman design.

General Electric Company (GEC): made light bulbs (later Osram bulbs) and switches etc., was greatly involved in the war effort, producing arc lights and work lamps, but the company also turned out some stylish Edwardian-style wall fittings and torchères.

Joseph Hinks & Son, Birmingham: patented the duplex burner and extinguisher lever in 1865. This worked better than a single-wick burner and the idea was copied by others when the patent expired. They also introduced a key to raise the gallery to make it easier to light the burner without having to remove the glass chimney.

Kynoch Ltd., Witton, England: originally a nineteenth-century candleworks, the firm diversified to lamps and eventually paraffin pressure stoves.

Samuel Messenger & Sons, Birmingham: founded around the mid 1830s, the firm produced candelabra, chandeliers and gas fittings, and exhibited in the 1851 Great Exhibition. The Messenger Model No 2 was a duplex burner with concentric wick-winder shafts.

This English paraffin/kerosene lamp shows the key for the Hinks No 2 duplex burner made by Joseph Hinks & Son of Birmingham.

W.H. Tilley, London: established in the early 1800s, specialising in practical, low-cost pressure lamps. At one time they manufactured gas fittings with an owl trademark. Their famous X246 lantern was first produced in 1946 in London and Belfast. Tilley still manufactures the Tilley Storm Light and can still provide parts for old lamps.

W. Tonks & Sons: founded by William Tonks in Birmingham, England in 1789. The firm won gold medals at the 1851 Great Exhibition in London, the 1855 *Exposition Internationale* in Paris, and the Great London Exposition in 1862. It manufactured architectural hardware, art metalware, campaign metalware, ecclesiastical metalwork and decorative patterned tubes. Its 1890 catalogue had over sixty pages, detailing a huge variety of hardware and domestic items.

The Valor Co., Birmingham: founded in 1901, famous for oil lamps and stoves.

This paraffin/kerosene lamp would have been considered adequate light for most domestic situations such as reading, playing the piano, needlework and entertaining a small number of guests.

Willis and Bates, Yorkshire: founded in the nineteenth century by Alfred Bates, they manufactured lighting units for GEC and Holophane Ltd. and for Tilley. The Vapalux trade name was registered in 1938 for their own pressure lamps (still made by Bairstow Bros (1985) Ltd.).

Young's Paraffin Light and Mineral Oil Co., Glasgow and Birmingham: Dr James Young started the first plant to produce paraffin from shale oil in 1848 and manufactured lamps and lamp burners.

Europe

Ehrich & Graetz, Germany: Adolf and Max Graetz were appointed managing directors of the family business in 1889. They developed the Petromax lantern, a pressurised, multi-fuel lantern designed to run on a variety of fuels including kerosene, alcohol-based fuels, mineral spirits, citronella oil, gasoline, diesel oil; in fact almost every flammable fuel available. Used by the German Army not just to produce light, but also to warm the troops with radiated heat. There was also a food-warmer lantern with a flat top on which to warm up the army rations. Eventually the lantern was renamed AIDA and all AIDA parts were interchangeable with Petromax parts. Later the name was changed again to the Geniol and again, all parts for all the lamps were interchangeable.

J.P. Kayser & Sohn, Krefeld, Germany: this small pewter foundry run by Jean Kayser was devoted to mass production. At the world exhibitions in Paris in 1900, Turin in 1902, Dusseldorf and St Louis in 1904, the company had great success with its introduction of 'Kayserzinn' or 'Kayser pewter', a special lead-free alloy of tin and silver distinguished by its lasting gleam. It was the Kayser Company's aim through its use of mass production to make artistically designed, contemporary *Jugendstil* objects of daily use such as candlesticks, lamps and other domestic products available to a broad section of the public. Kayserzinn objects are marked with the word Kayserzinn and given a number.

Lempreur & Bernard, Lampes Belges, Belgium: makers of paraffin lamps and gas fittings with characteristic circular burners. Trade mark 'L&B' and a sun seen on the wick-winder.

NICS Frères: French brothers Michel and Jules, artist ironsmiths who produced a wide range of ironwork, especially all sorts of light fittings in the 1920s. They made many of the wrought iron fittings for Daum's glass lamps and chandeliers.

Orivit: German art metalware company in the early 1900s producing table lamps in silvered bronze as well as candlesticks and candelabra in bronze and pewter.

Osiris: German pewter foundry producing fine art metalware including candlesticks, lamps and other small decorative items from 1906.

Wild & Wessel, Berlin: the company worked in bronze and created the Kosmos, an improved and highly successful oil-burner.

The USA
The Mantle Lamp Company of America: (later Aladdin), USA (see p. 77).

American Gas Light Co., Minnesota: Hans Hanson (eventually known as 'Gas' Hanson) was born in Denmark and moved to America when he was about 10 years old. Towards the end of the 1800s he began experimenting with gasoline as a fuel and was making lighting appliances by 1896. He formed a partnership with Thomas Hjort to create the American Gas Light Company and became a strong competitor to Coleman, selling lights for indoor and outdoor use. Within ten years his American Gas Light Co. was producing high-quality lamps for homes and farms.

Archer Pancoast, New York: a leading major firm of gas lighting and early electric light fixtures during the late 1800s. Edward F. Caldwell, a portrait painter, became chief designer and vice president of the company. He was producing designs that mastered the new technology while adapting electric lamps to the traditional ornamental aesthetics suitable to nineteenth-century American taste. In 1895 Caldwell established his own firm, Edward F. Caldwell & Co. Inc. of New York with Victor von Lossberg, designer and craftsman. They frequently travelled to Europe to study and import historic lamps as inspiration for their fixtures. They were known for producing lighting fixtures and metalwork objects in high-quality bronze, iron, silver, brass and copper. Most designs were based on traditional styles.

Bradley & Hubbard: Walter Hubbard and his brother-in-law Nathaniel Lyman Bradley started making cast-iron clocks, tables, brass, andirons, lamps, chandeliers, sconces and sewing-machines in 1854. After 1900 they began to produce electric lamps, inspired by Tiffany, with mosaic glass shades on bronze and brass bases. They also made shades of iridescent glass blown into bronze or brass forms. The Charles Parker Company bought the company in 1840.

Bridgeport Brass Co., Brooklyn: founded in 1865 to make clock movements but eventually produced a variety of brass items including lamps, lamp-burners and trimmings, electric lamp sockets and much more. The company was assigned at least forty-five light-related patents between 1868 and 1909.

Charles Parker Company, Meriden, Connecticut: produced brass and iron foundry products (including the famous Parker Brothers Shotguns), such as tables, sewing-machines, andirons, lamps, chandeliers and sconces.

Coleman Lamp Company, Kansas: in the 1890s William Coleman was a salesman for typewriters in Alabama when he came across the 'Efficient Lamp', a pendant arc lamp manufactured by the Irby and Gilliland Company. He was astonished by its brilliant white light and immediately signed on as a salesman with the company. He went on to form his own Hydro-Carbon Light Company which later became the Coleman Lamp Company. In 1914 the company introduced the Coleman Arc Lantern, the lantern that made it famous. At 300 cp it could light the far corners of a barn and provide good light in every direction for 100 yards. It was declared an 'essential item' and over 70,000 were distributed across the nation, allowing farmers and workers to extend their hours and produce items essential to the war effort. Design and development proceeded to the

Brass reflected the light and was well suited to such lamps as this wall bracket.

first match-light lantern, the Quick-Lite in 1916, to Instant-Lite lamps and lanterns burning petroleum, then to paraffin/kerosene versions. Glass and fabric were used for indoor shades and mica for outdoor lanterns.

Cornelius & Baker, Philadelphia: famous for chandeliers during the second half of the nineteenth century.

Irby and Gilliland Company, Alabama: made 'The Efficient' pendant arc lamp; later the company was purchased by W.C. Coleman.

Manhattan Brass Company, Manhattan, New York: this company is probably best known for its Perfection Student Lamps, but it also made brass bicycle lamps and flat-wick burners. The student lamps were made in various sizes using 7- and 10-in shades in single and double versions. They could also be wall-mounted. The company was assigned many lighting-related patents between 1879 and 1910, and closed in 1926.

Miller, Edward & Company: US manufacturer of decorative metal objects including oil lamp bases during the late nineteenth century, based in Connecticut. Later the company started producing a range of metal table lamps and ceiling fittings with ornate mosaic opaline glass shades in the style of Tiffany.

Mitchell, Vance & Co., New York: had a showroom in Broadway and a factory on Tenth Avenue in the late 1800s manufacturing gas fixtures and ornamental metalwork.

Rochester Lamp Co.: founded in 1844 by Charles Stanford Upton using a patent for improved air distribution in centre-draft lamps. Rochester lamps were made from 1884–92 by Edward Miller and thereafter as 'New Rochester Lamps' by The Bridgeport Brass Co.

Roycroft Community, East Aurora, New York: made many interesting pieces including leaded glass lamps and copper shade lamps between 1909 and 1926.

Glass used for lighting

The earliest glass lampshades were generally made in the shapes of vases. They had openings both at the bottom

A rococo brass candlestick with a carrying handle, designed to be used only in the best rooms or for visitors, as such a candlestick would have been expensive.

The Roycroft Community

Elbert Hubbard was an entrepreneur who started off selling soap. In the early 1840s he gave up conventional business, went to Harvard but dropped out and travelled to Europe where he met William Morris and was inspired by the ideas of the Arts and Crafts movement.

He started a printing business, then bought property in East Aurora and established an Arts and Crafts community which he called The Roycroft. Between 1896 and 1910 he established a bindery, a print shop, a powerhouse, a chapel and a blacksmith's shop – a whole variety of buildings similar to a college campus.

His intention was that talented craftspeople would come to the Roycroft Community, learn skills and sell products. It was a self-sustaining individual craft community. Around 1908 the blacksmith's shop became the copper shop where a group of talented craftsmen produced work. In the early days, everything was given a simple brown finish.

When Victor Toothaker joined the community in 1912, the metalwork expanded and the workshop started making a full line of lamps and vases. Later a brass finish was introduced and later still Aurora brown lacquer finish, a Verde green and an Etruscan green, an acid-etched finish and a silver finish. During the 1920s a strong influence was brought in particularly by Dard Hunter and Karl Kipp, reflecting the avant garde Vienna Secession designs that were happening in Austria and England. Although there were several hundred people in the Roycroft Community there were never more than about thirty working in the copper shop. Almost all Roycroft pieces are marked which makes identification easier.

and at the top. The bottom of the glass covering was fitted to a lamp which was either filled with whale oil or with camphene. The air from the openings helped the lamp to shine brighter. The glass covering shaded the lamp from outside draughts. Gradually different fuels were used to light lamps. The glass covering was bulged around the wick because most of the air that supported the flame was stored there. The shades on kerosene and paraffin lamps were taller and narrower in shape without the bulge. The long, narrow shape pulled the flame towards the top, making it more powerful and bright. This shape was carried into the twentieth century but during the whole of the nineteenth century ornate glass lampshades with floral imagery grew in popularity and began to become decorative objects in their own right. Slag glass (pressed glass with milky stripes) became popular in England and America and many companies produced astonishing works of art in their glass shades. By the nineteenth century the names of individual designers and manufacturers of chandeliers began to be acknowledged. In England there were the White House Glass Works; Baccarat in France; Schonbek and Swarovski in Czechoslovakia; Lobmeyer in Austria; the Mount Washington Glass Factory (Pairpoint) in America and many more.

Tiffany had an enormous influence on the design of art glass lamps in the USA and in Europe. Copies of his ideas, sometimes excellent and sometimes garish, abound. This lamp is typical of the better designs, being both elegant and jewel-like.

As electricity became cheaper and more widely used, glass shades were used to lessen the glare so that the lamps emitted soothing, soft light. The shapes of these lamps no longer depended on the efficient burning of a liquid fuel and much effort went into creating different, modern, glass coverings for electric lamps. The glass was stained with beautiful colours and many fantastic decorations were incorporated, as in Tiffany's extraordinary lamps.

Some common types of glass

Cameo glass (also verre double)

This is one of the most skilled products of glassmaking. Basically it is any glass on which the surface is cut away to leave a design in relief. It may be clear or coloured glass, a single layer or multiple layers fused together, clear or coloured. The cutting away of a portion of glass can be done with hand cutting tools like those used by sculptors in other media, or it may be cut by a wheel or hydrofluoric acid. The term cabochon refers to applied bits of glass which have the appearance of jewels and which may have carving on the surface.

Cameo glass appeared in England in 1876. The removal of the 1845 tax on glass encouraged innovation and allowed for experimentation and progress. At Stourbridge, where the English glass industry had been centred since the seventeenth century, Thomas Webb, Benjamin Richardson and William Haden Richardson formed the Wordsley Glass Works in 1836. For forty years Benjamin Richardson was responsible for encouraging many great glass craftsmen in producing cameo glass. In the last half of the nineteenth century tiny copper wheels and steel gravers made it possible for the manufacturers of Stourbridge to create much more detailed work.

A pair of small cranberry glass paraffin/kerosene lamps that could look charming at either end of a mantelpiece, or on a dresser or sideboard.

Case glass (also overlay glass)

Made up of two layers of glass with the inside white to reflect more light and the outside coloured; green and white was a common combination. There were different types of art glass shades including satin, amberina, cranberry and mother-of-pearl.

Cranberry glass

The glass which is known today as cranberry glass was probably first produced in Bohemia in the early eighteenth century, though in those days it was known as ruby glass. This delicate glass was made with a thin layer of red glass in or outside a thicker layer of clear glass. There was a tremendous growth in design and style throughout the nineteenth century around the period of the Great Exhibition. The heyday of cranberry glass was from 1870–1930 by which time it was being produced in England, France, Belgium, Bavaria and Bohemia, as well as in the United States. The glassworks in America were mainly in New England which is where cranberries are grown, and that's how it acquired its present name.

Craquelé glass

A thick glass with a crackled outside finish, often used to make globes for Art Deco figure lamps.

Crystal glass

A transparent glass of a high degree of brilliance and optical purity, used in chandeliers in the form of droplets appreciated for its decorative beauty which comes from the refraction of light passing through a prism – in the same way that rainbows are formed.

Flakestone glass

A marbled-effect opaque glass often used in the 1930s, especially for lampshades.

Holophane glass

Glass used for lampshades made up of tiny prisms to help direct and magnify a light source, used in gas, oil or electric lighting. Holophane shades had vertical internal flutings and horizontal external flutings, the forms of which were calculated so that each part of the globe sent some light to all parts of the space surrounding the light source. They were also designed to reduce the loss of light caused by absorption and internal reflections in the glass itself.

In the United States manufacturers such as Westmoreland and Akro Agate also used the techniques to produce their own versions of slag glass. As in England, one of the most popular uses for this glass was lampshades. Creamy colours allowed the light in the lamp to give a soft glow.

This Holophane lampshade was designed for use in a factory. The Holophane shade is made of prisms which magnify and diffuse the light, giving an efficient and undazzling illumination.

Lamp chimney glass

Early lamp chimneys were all hand-blown, free-form and finished by glass-blowers. At some point moulds were introduced to get a consistent form but they were still created by hand. Later the whole process was mechanised. The chimneys might be plain glass, or etched or embossed.

Le Verre Français

One of many types of cameo glass made by the Schneider Glassworks in France. The glass was made by the C. Schneider factory in Epinay-sur-Seine from 1918 to 1933. It is a mottled glass, usually decorated with floral designs and carries the incised signature *Le Verre Français.*

Milk glass

Milk glass is an opaque or translucent glass, blown or pressed in a wide variety of shapes. Plain opal shades were made with milk glass which was utilitarian and inexpensive. It was first made in Venice in the sixteenth century. The white colour is achieved by adding something to make the glass opaque, such as bone ash or tin dioxide and it can come in other colours too.

Milk glass globes were used a great deal in early factory lighting. Like Holophane glass, they diffused the light without diminishing it too much, giving a clear but comfortable general light. (Photo: Trainspotters)

Murano glass

The beginning of the Murano glass-blowing tradition probably began around the tenth century. The island of Murano was part of the young republic of Venice. Murano became a centre for glass when all foundries around Venice itself were ordered to move to the island because of fire hazard to the city. Murano glassmakers were allowed to wear swords, had immunity from prosecution by the Venetian state and married their daughters into Venice's most affluent families. However, in order to safeguard the glass manufacturing and blowing techniques, glassmakers were not allowed to leave the Venetian Republic. Glass-blowers who shared their working techniques with other countries were punished. The island relied almost entirely on its glass business for its economy and Murano held a monopoly on glass-making for hundreds of years, developing or refining many technologies including crystalline glass, enamelled glass (smalto), glass with threads of gold (aventurine), multicoloured glass (millefiori), milk glass (lattimo), and imitation gemstones made of glass.

A good example of Murano glass comes from Venice itself where the glass has been used for centuries in wonderfully attractive street lighting.

Opalescent glass

Generalised term for a clear and semi-opaque pressed glass which is cloudy, marbled and sometimes subtly coloured, combining to form a milky opalescence produced in the cooling process. It is also produced by alternating heating and cooling of the glass and with the addition of chemical additives to create different effects. John La Farge and Louis Comfort Tiffany were two American artists who first experimented with opalescent effects. In England Davidson's was the major European manufacturer, marketing their opalescent glass as Pearline. One type of opalescent glass is tinged blue with a milky opalescence at its centre, typical of Lalique, Sabino and other European manufacturers.

Opaline glass

A semi-opaque translucent glass produced in England and France during the nineteenth and early twentieth centuries. When held to the light, many pieces produce warm rosy hues. It was made in pastel colours, often with special effects of iridescent and translucent colours.

Overlay glass

See case glass.

Pressed glass

Made by using a plunger to press molten glass into a mould, it was developed in the United States from the 1820s and in Europe particularly in France, Bohemia and Sweden from the 1830s.

Rock crystal

A natural quartz prized by collectors since ancient times. Billions of years in its formation make each crystal unique. The raw crystal is mined, not manufactured. It cannot be mass-produced. Skilled gem cutters grind, cut and polish each rock crystal by hand. Polishing one crystal to perfection can take a week.

Satin glass

The name for any glass that has been chemically treated to give it a satin finish. It is often used to refer to a collectible type of pressed glass. The satin finish is produced by treating the glass with hydrofluoric acid. It was first made as decorative pressed glass in Europe and the United States during the 1880s. It is opaque and has decorative surface patterns moulded into it. It is often tinted with a pastel colour such as blue.

Slag glass

Also known as marble glass or malachite, this is a type of opaque, streaked pressed glass that originated in late nineteenth-century England where glass manufacturers are thought to have added slag from iron-smelting works to molten glass to create a range of effects from tortoiseshell to marbling. It was a

Slag glass was used by many of the art glass lamp manufacturers. This lamp could have been made by Handel & Company in Connecticut, which was well known for its slag glass shades.

popular material for lampshades and just about any designer producing lamps during the Art Nouveau period would use it. Makers from Tiffany to Roycroft and Steuben would probably have used slag glass in their shades and it became particularly popular during the 1930s and 40s. True slag glass is richly marbled rather than only streaked or coloured. One of the first companies to produce slag glass was the English firm of Sowerby in Gateshead which patented a recipe for purple malachite glass in 1878. It was used for lampshades and sold in the United States as 'blackberries and cream' and followed by other colours such as a lemon yellow called Giallo, a green called Pomona, a blue called Sorbini and Sowerby's famous Brown. The lamps made with slag glass had shades with glass panels that slotted into metal frames with different kinds of slots and clips. In many lamps the base was also decorated with glass panels with the metal design lying over part of the glass.

Spatter glass
An opaque glass speckled with brightly-coloured enamel glass.

Supastone
A popular glass for inverted burner shades, this was an opaque creamy-white three-ply glass consisting of a centre of opal glass with clear flint on the inside and polished satin on the outside. They gave an intense white light without glare, which was restful on the eyes. It was considered the best type of glass for ornamental looks and had smooth internal and external surfaces which were easy to clean. Supastone was either moulded into attractive self-patterns or carefully hand-painted with pretty floral scenes and other motifs by specialist artists. It was extensively used in shops, hotels, offices, theatres and public buildings, as well as for domestic lighting.

Vaseline glass
A term that should apply only to uranium glass which has a yellow or green appearance, but in the United Kingdom and Australia, the term vaseline glass can be used to refer to any type of translucent glass. Even within the United States, the vaseline description is sometimes applied to any type of translucent glass with a surface lustre.

Verre double
See cameo glass.

Glass for chandeliers
The first chandeliers, made of glass rather than rock crystal, were produced originally in Murano, an island just off Venice. Venetian crystal is moulded and fire-polished rather than cut, which results in a subtle luminosity rather than brilliance. Lead crystal, originally known as flint glass, was first patented by an Englishman, George Ravenscroft on behalf of the Worshipful Company of Glass Sellers in London in 1675. Said to be dissatisfied with the glass from Murano, he introduced lead, which made the glass highly refractive and so brighter with cut edges producing spectrums of colour. The ingredients were sand, potash, lead oxide and crushed flint and his patent described it as: 'A particuler sort of cristalline

A comparatively simple antique chandelier with candle-holders and a fringe of crystal droplets seen against an unashamedly decorative ceiling; the fitting has been converted to electricity.

Some notes on crystals

The crystals used in fine chandeliers are made of transparent glass. A crystal is like a diamond, and its value depends in the same way on the quality of the material and how it is cut. The fire and brilliance of a crystal come from the light passing through a prism (the same thing happens when light passes through raindrops to form a rainbow). The earliest known crystal chandeliers appeared in the sixteenth century and were made of rock crystal of irregular shapes. The idea was to increase the modest power of candlelight. By the seventeenth century craftsmen of the baroque era had perfected the art of cutting rock crystal for chandeliers and the antique shapes designed at the time are still in use today. Crystal today may be machine-cut, hand-cut or moulded.

An example of the ways in which crystals could be strung in necklace-like lengths; each chain with small droplets ending in a heavier globular pendant.

In the late 1800s Daniel Swarovski of Austria began a career in stone-cutting and crystal manufacture. Swarovski patented a machine to cut jewellery stones and expanded the use of this technology to include cutting crystal chandelier pieces. He perfected the purity of leaded glass crystal to a state of flawless brilliance. Swarovski crystal is still considered the best in the world.

Five main types of crystal:

- **Rock crystal**: this is not glass at all but a type of rock (quartz) mined from the ground. Each individual crystal has taken over 1 billion years to form. Rock crystal is cool to the touch, no matter what the ambient temperature.
- **Vintage crystal**: crystals found in antique chandeliers, often in old-fashioned shapes such as little beads, droplets, antique-style faceted ovals, chains of fanciful beading or octagons.
- **Legacy crystals**: these come from glass-making regions in and around Venice

A simple chandelier with raised arms to hold the candles, now converted to electricity but still giving a bright, lively, sparkling light through its droplets.

including Murano. Venetian crystal is moulded and fire-polished rather than cut, which results in subtle luminosity rather than brilliance.

- **Hand-cut crystal**: each crystal is cut by hand in two stages, first on an iron and then a sandstone wheel. Each crystal is then hand-polished on a wooden wheel with marble dust.
- **Swarovski crystal**: the finest crystal, manufactured in the Austrian Alps and extremely clear and flawless with a unique purity and brilliance, characterised by razor-sharp machine-cut facets. The lead content is more than 30 per cent.

glasse resembling rock christall.' He discovered that the addition of lead oxide also made the glass softer and easier to cut.

By 1720 lead crystal chandeliers had begun to appear, although they were often referred to as branches or lustres. Two successful English manufacturers of chandeliers in the Georgian period were William Parker and Jonathan Collet. Georgian crystal is often recognised by its blue-grey tint, being mined in Derbyshire and known as Derby Blue, but by 1816 manufacturers were adding purified lead oxide instead, which eliminated the tint. Eventually the manufacture of crystal glass spread to Bohemia, Spain, England and Ireland. By the nineteenth century, Bohemia (site of the first Schonbek crystal factory) had become the world's leading producer of fine crystal.

A very different chandelier relying on its intricate crystals to reflect light and to sparkle from all their various points.

Some influential early glass/lamp manufacturers

Britain

F. & C. Osler, Birmingham: founded in 1807 by Thomas Osler and later joined by his sons Thomas Clarkson Osler and A. Follet Osler, the company became one of the best-known glassmakers in the world, sending chandeliers to India, Persia and America. The company thrived on the production of ornate chandeliers and massive glass structures (including staircases, tables and thrones) until 1914. Their success was largely due to A.F. Osler's development of a method of building up

A beautifully cut crystal ball – the final droplet for a highly ornate crystal chandelier.

solid glass around a metal core, creating objects of a size and complexity previously thought impossible.

Parker, William: in 1771, William Parker, glassmaker of Fleet Street, London leaped into prominence when he supplied all the chandeliers except one for the new Assembly Rooms in Bath. All these chandeliers are still in the rooms. He also patented a type of base for candelabra and in 1782 supplied girandoles to the Duke of Devonshire at Chatsworth.

Perry & Co.: in 1817 William Perry set up his own workshop in London as 'Glass manufacturer to the Prince Regent'. In 1822 he was joined by his nephew George and in 1833 with the arrival of another family member, the firm was renamed Perry & Co. which became one of the leading glassmakers of the nineteenth century, responsible for some magnificent chandeliers notably for the Duke of Devonshire at Chatsworth and the Worshipful Company of Goldsmiths.

Crystals were often used on candlesticks and there are many Victorian candlesticks with long cut-glass prisms which can be quite appropriate in today's modern interiors.

Ravenscroft, George: in 1675, said to be dissatisfied with the glass from Murano, he introduced lead, which made the glass highly refractive and so brighter with cut edges producing spectrums of colour. The ingredients were sand, potash, lead oxide and crushed flint and his patent described it as: 'A particuler sort of cristalline glasse resembling rock christall.' He discovered that the addition of lead oxide also made the glass softer and easier to cut (see p. 127).

William Sugg: in 1875 William Sugg was making a wide range of albatrine (a white, translucent glass, similar to opal glass) globes, round in shape but open at the top with a smaller opening at the bottom which fitted into galleries on their Christiana burners. These shades, in pretty opaque opal-coloured glass were similar to oil lamps shades of the time and were hand-painted by French artists in soft colours with motifs taken mostly from nature including children, flowers, trees, birds, animals and peaceful countryside and fishing scenes. When lit, the pictures appeared to come magically to life.

Europe
Baccarat: during the nineteenth century Baccarat was a leading French manufacturer of pressed glass and also made tableware and lamps. The firm's high-quality work looked very like blown cut glass.

Bagues Frères, Paris, France: in the 1930s the brothers Bagues produced a wide variety of lighting fixtures and ironwork in both modern Art Deco pieces and reproductions of antique light fittings, particularly Louis XIV and Empire styles. They elaborated and mixed the two, using flowers, fruit and animals for their subjects. Their preferred materials were clear or opalescent glass beads and rock crystals set in silvered or gilt mounts. They made some stunning chandeliers.

Daum: in 1878 Jean Daum, a French notary, took over a glass factory in Nancy, in lieu of a debt. The Daums used many techniques developed by Émile Gallé, but also developed some of their own techniques and their own artistic style. As they were money men rather than artists, they hired the best artists including Charles Schneider – although all the work was signed 'Daum'. The firm is perhaps best known for its acid-cut work with enamel and bold decoration which is their more typical style and accounts for a large portion of their cameo glass production. The family continued to produce candlesticks, lamp bases and other items until 1981 when the factory was taken over by CFC Compagnie du Cristal.

Degue: David Gueron Degue was of Turkish origin but came to France and in 1926 he set up his glassworks, the *Verrerie d'Art Degue* to produce luxury art glass which included vases, lamps and chandeliers. His work was full of deep colours especially red, orange and green, which he achieved with a special process. He produced several different styles of chandelier lighting, all with the thick glass for which it is known and various hand-worked metals. The bowl was usually suspended by three silk cords or three nickel or chrome rods with a metal ceiling canopy. Each light was usually illuminated by a simple bulb suspended just above the glass bowl. As well as his own designs he is said to have copied those of other glassworks of the time, particularly those of Schneider.

Gallé: Émile Gallé (1874) owned the *Cristallerie d'Émile Gallé* where he produced complex and intricate glass designs that took days of painstaking effort. He worked with cameo glass in particular and, as a botanist, his designs were inspired by nature with insects, flowers, dragonflies and dew on leaves as popular themes. He won many awards throughout his working life including the French *Légion d'Honneur* and was an influence on many of the artist craftsmen of his day including Tiffany. In 1897 Gallé introduced a technique which he called *marqueterie de verre*.

This sky-blue glass pendant shade was made in France for electric lighting in the late nineteenth or early twentieth century. (Seen at the Salvo Fair 2010)

He pressed semi molten glass into the surface of the blank before cooling produced the design. The glass could then be carved. If the carving produced a design in relief, then this carved portion might be considered as cameo. *Pate de verre* (glass paste) is not cameo but a type of glass in which powdered glass is moulded and then fused by heating. *Pate de verre* was produced in antiquity and the technique was revived in the latter part of the nineteenth century. In the late 1800s and 1900s there were a number of people who used this technique in at least some of their work, including Émile Gallé and the Daum brothers.

Lalique: René Jules Lalique was famous for his exquisite perfume bottles, vases, jewellery and clocks, and also for chandeliers. At the age of 16 he was apprenticed to a Parisian jeweller, Louis Aucoc. He attended an English art college for two years and when he returned to France worked for several top jewellers. In 1882 he became a freelance designer for several jewellery houses in Paris and four years later established his own jewellery workshop. By 1890 he had become one of France's foremost Art Nouveau jewellery designers, creating pieces for Samuel Bing's Paris shop *La Maison de l'Art Nouveau*. In the 1920s he became famous for his work in the Art Deco style and was responsible for the walls of lighted glass and elegant glass columns which filled the dining room and grand salon of the SS *Normandie*. Lampshades created by Lalique are delightful objects in their own right and emit a gentle, magical glow.

Legras & Cie: an important glassworks founded by Auguste J.F. Legras in Saint-Denis near Paris. The firm produced a wide range of glassware including a series of table lamps in etched and cased glass with pastoral scenes or natural landscapes. They used soft autumnal colours and cameo and enamel painting and were frequently mistaken for the lamps of Gallé. They closed down during World War One and reopened as the *Verreries et Cristalleries de St Denis et de Pantin Réunis*.

Loetz Witwe, Johann: Austrian glassworks founded in 1836 and acquired by Johann Loetz in 1840. His grandson Max Ritter took over in 1879, turning it into one of the most important and influential glassworks in Europe. By the 1880s the company was making multicoloured inlays and iridescent glass and supplying crude glass to Tiffany in New York.

Muller Frères: the Muller Brothers worked for Gallé before they established their glassworks at Luneville. Later glass production was moved to Croismare, a short distance away. Most of the glass produced at Luneville was signed Muller Frères Luneville or Muller, or Luneville. At Croismare glass was signed Muller Croismare, Muller, Croismare, Muller Croismare Nancy or Croismare Nancy. At Luneville cameo glass was produced almost entirely by acid-cutting. A greater variety of styles is evident in the Croismare cameo pieces, with both acid- and wheel-cutting used.

Perzel, Jean, Paris: Jean Perzel moved to Paris when he was 10 and later set up a glassmaking business in 1892. Although originally trained to paint stained glass, Perzel became world-famous for designing and manufacturing exclusive light fittings. His lamps were extremely modern, highly functional and designed to maximise the light while still diffusing it. He developed special glass tinted pink or beige to transmit the light uniformly. He achieved international renown and prestigious commissions to design and provide the light fittings for the United Nations Building, Geneva; Luxembourg cathedral; the Henry Ford Building, Detroit; the Savoy Hotel, London; the palace of the King of Siam; the Maharaja's residence in Indor; and the luxury ocean liner SS *Normandie*.

This delicate frilly pendant flower of transparent glass was made in France probably in the early twentieth century and has a porcelain-weighted rise-and-fall mechanism. (Seen at the Salvo Fair 2010)

Rousseau and Leveille: Eugene Rousseau produced layered glass and did some engraving in glass surfaces in about 1884 and 1885. Rousseau pieces are rare and unless signed may be difficult to attribute with any certainty.

Sabino Glass, Paris: Sabino Glass was set up after World War One to make glass products such as lampshades, lamps, glass panels for electric lighting and a range of opalescent glass vases and statuettes. He used pressed and moulded glass, decorating it with motifs of flowers and fruits as well as more abstract designs of waves, rain and cascades. 'Verart' and 'Vernox' were two trademarks used by Sabino during the 1930s for glass developed to compete with companies like Holophane producing cheaper glass. He produced anything that could be illuminated indoors and out, including lamps for the SS *Normandie* and for many hotels and restaurants. He became particularly well-known for his larger creations. The company had a workshop and retail outlet in Paris and won prizes at all the major international exhibitions between the two world wars. In 1975 the entire Sabino operation (moulds, factory, designs, rights and glass formulae) was sold to the company's American agent and his Sabino Crystal Company carried on producing Sabino's Art Glass in France using the original manufacturing processes and designs.

Schneider: Charles Schneider was born in 1881 and apprenticed to the renowned firm of Daum Frères. In 1909 he and his brother Ernest bought an electric light bulb factory in Epinay-sur-Seine, which closed when the brothers joined the army in 1914. The factory reopened in 1917 under the name *Societé Anonyme des Verreries Schneider*. With Charles as the design genius it produced exquisite Art Nouveau cameo glass bowls, vases and lamps in bright colours with floral and animal designs.

In 1918, when fire destroyed the Gallé workshop, a group of artists joined Schneider to continue production for Gallé. Schneider was thus able to learn the technique of *marqueterie de verre* from them. This was similar to marquetry in wood where the design was carved out of a piece of glass and filled with coloured glass. *Le verre français* was made using the acid-etching technique, which could produce good quality work at a reasonable price. The technique of wheel-engraving was used only for special pieces. In 1924 the brothers moved into a larger factory with modern furnaces and more employees, and changed the name to *Verrerie Schneider*. Charles, always innovative, developed a technique of using coloured powder whereby pulverised glass was mixed with metal oxides to obtain different colours and blown onto a flat surface, in layers. Most of his lamps and vases were exported to the USA and the factory closed in 1981.

Schonbek: Adolf Schonbek formed his own glassworks in 1870 and concentrated on manufacturing chandeliers. He is said to have built his first chandelier by hand, sitting in a rented basement flat. He built up a highly successful company which continued in business until World War Two. After the war his five factories in Czechoslovakia were taken over by the communist regime and he left to start his business up in Canada and later, New York where the family still owns and controls the chandelier business.

The USA
Many of the most successful companies producing Art Nouveau lamps were started by people who had worked for Tiffany and had left to create their own businesses.

Consolidated Lamp and Glass Co. of Coraopolis, Pennsylvania (formerly the Fostoria Shade and Lamp Company): produced highly decorative paraffin/kerosene lamps from the late 1890s to 1915.

This decorated opal art glass parlour vase lamp has its original Fostoria High Grade trim. It is 26in tall with a stencilled and painted ball shade in Lady and the Swan pattern. Manufactured around the turn of the twentieth century. (Photo: 19th Century Lighting Co.)

Duffner & Kimberly: comparatively small output and much of the work was unsigned; however, they did introduce a circular locking mechanism whereby the shade is secured on top of the base, which can help to identify a Duffner & Kimberly lamp.

Fostoria Glass Co., West Virginia: fine art glass producers from the early 1900s. From 1900 they specialised in coloured lustre glass, marketed under the trademark IRIS. They manufactured table lamps with illuminated bases of blown glass and shades for oil and electric lights. Fostoria was taken over by GEC of New York and closed in 1917.

Handel & Company, Meriden, Connecticut (1893–1936): the company originally produced a general range of domestic glassware such as vases and tobacco jars. Later Philip Handel began producing lamps. The company bought up sheet glass, cut up the sheets into individual pieces and made them up into floral or geometric lampshades or decorated the blank with filigree metal overlays and applied a 'chipped' finish to the outside surface of the shade. Nearly all the work was signed and they turned out a huge volume of shades, at first specialising in reverse painted lampshades, painted on the inside of the glass creating three-dimensional-looking images. Their Art Nouveau designs were very popular, designed and decorated by Handel's studio of artists and craftsmen and similar to those produced by Tiffany, but less expensive. However, the company found it difficult to adapt to Art Deco and closed in 1936.

Holophane Company: in the 1890s in America the Holophane Glass Company was created to manufacture prismatic 'illuminating appliances'. The company was founded by André Blondel, a French scientist and Spiridon Psaroudaki, a Greek engineer, who patented their invention in 1839. They made glass globes with horizontal parallel prisms positioned to control the light. Many were exported to Europe. 'Holophane' from the Greek 'holos' (whole) and 'phaneir' (to appear) means to appear completely luminous. By the 1920s there were several Holophane companies manufacturing economical lighting for large factories. The most famous Holophane installation is probably the supplemental lights installed in 1937 in Westminster Abbey for the coronation of George VI and the floodlighting for the exterior of the Abbey and the House of Lords and famously the lighting for Radio City Studios in New York and for street lighting. Individual lamps, pendant or free-standing from redundant factories are much sought after for retro twentieth-century interiors.

Moran & Hastings: US manufacturing company specialising in electric lights and fittings in the Tiffany style during the early 1900s.

Pairpoint Manufacturing Company: the Mt Washington Glass Company was founded in 1837 in South Washington. In 1889 it merged with Pairpoint Manufacturing, a silver and metalworks company founded by Thomas Pairpoint. The company began designing interesting complete lamps using glass or mixed metal and glass. These metal-based lamps feature ornate, polychrome glass shades and are highly collectible. Lava, Peachglow and Satin glass were first created by Pairpoint glass-blowers. They also developed a type of art glass called 'tulip glass' designed by Albert Steffin and patented for Pairpoint in 1908. Pairpoint is the oldest operating glassworks in the country. Examples of their designs can be found in the decorative arts collections of the Metropolitan Museum of Art in New York and the Boston Museum of Fine Arts. The most easily identifiable glass Pairpoint shade is known as 'puffy' because glass was blown into plump forms shaped like flower petals before they were painted inside.

Peters, H.J.: US manufacturer of leaded glass and bent panelled lampshades in Tiffany style in the early 1900s.

Pittsburgh Lamp, Brass & Glass Company, Pittsburgh, Pennsylvania: operated from c.1900 to 1915 making art glass lamps including miniature night lamps.

Quezal: Martin Bach and Thomas Johnson both worked for Tiffany before setting up their business; one as a batch-mixer and the other as a gaffer. Although they copied his designs, the Quezal workmanship was always excellent.

Steuben: initially set up to make the glass blanks and crystal ware for the glass-cutting company T.G. Hawkes & Co. The firm appointed an Englishman Frederick Carder as its art director. The company began to make small hand-blown light fixtures, small table lamps, branched chandeliers consisting of several single-bulb shades, and candlesticks. Motifs included feathers and trailing lily pads.

Tiffany, Louis Comfort: best known for his Favrile shades, researched into iridescence, mottling and incandescence.

Other manufacturers who produced leaded glass similar to Tiffany's included Carl V. Helmschmied Manufacturing Co.; the US Art Bent Glass Co. in Connecticut; Williamson and Co.; the Moran and Hastings Manufacturing Co. all of Chicago; and the Albert Sechrist Manufacturing Co. of Denver. Lamps from all these companies and others like them can still be found for sale.

This green satin patterned art glass night lamp with a 'square base drape' pattern was manufactured by the Pittsburgh Lamp, Brass & Glass Company to light a boudoir or bedroom. (Photo: 19th Century Lighting Co.)

Porcelain manufacturers who made lamps

Glass was the most popular material for lamps and shades from early on but in Europe porcelain was used for some early paraffin/kerosene lamps, for candle-holders of various sorts and for later electric lights and, of course, many early lamps have been adapted to electricity. Some were moulded into sculptured shapes with putti (cherubs), as well as fruit and flowers. Others were in simple rounded shapes with applied decoration, again with flowers and fruit. A number of Chinese, Japanese and European porcelain vases have been adapted to create modern electric lamps but the main European porcelain manufacturers of figurines, dinner sets, vases and urns turned their hand to lamps as well. The mark KPM was used by many German porcelain makers including the famous Meissen factory. It stands for *Königliche Porzellan-Manufaktur* (Royal Porcelain Manufactury). Famous porcelain producers include Meissen (Dresden); Gebrüder Schoenau (Thuringia); Potschappel (Dresden); Von Schierholz (Dresden); and Klöpfel & Sons (Ehrfurt).

Pierrot became a popular motif for lamps in the nineteenth century and some manufacturers made a speciality of them. This one holds a milk glass globe in his lap which, when switched on, lights up his masked face and porcelain ruff. (Photo: Louise Verber, Alfie's Antique Market)

Some influential twentieth-century manufacturers of 'designer' lights

Arredoluce (Italian): founded by Angelo Lelli in the 1950s; worked with such designers as Achille Castiglioni and Ettore Sottsass.

Arteluce (Italian): aeronaval engineer Gino Sarfatti worked on lighting design and set up Arteluce in 1939. The company soon became a national and international influence on modern lighting design and won numerous prizes and awards including the *Compasso d'Oro* in 1954 and 1955. Arteluce became a centre of excellence and a meeting-place and forum for many of the leading Italian designers of the 1950s and 60s.

Artemide (Italian): founded by Ernesto Gismondi and Sergio Mazza in 1858 in Milan. Best known for the Tizio desk lamp designed by Richard Sapper in 1972 and the Tolomeo desk lamp by Michele de Lucchi and Giancarlo Fassina in 1986. Other designers who collaborated with the company include Mario Botta, Ettore Sottsass and Sir Norman Foster.

Best & Lloyd (British): Best & Lloyd began making brass components in 1840. By 1900 it had become one of the most prestigious suppliers of chandeliers to public buildings in Europe and America. In 1930 it launched the Best Lite, designed by Robert Dudley Best, inspired by his studies at the Dusseldorf School of Industrial Design and his friendship with Walter Gropius, principal of the Bauhaus School. The Best Lite is a masterpiece of classic simplicity, still in production in Birmingham by the Danish company Gubi.

Claus Bolby (Scandinavian): designer/manufacturer who designed the Symfoni in the 1960s and worked on variations for the next ten years in his own workshop and sold through retailers.

Flos Lighting (Italian): in 1959 Arturo Eisenkeil, an importer of Cocoon (a spray-on plastic coating produced in the United States), was looking for possible applications for this new material. He set up a company to create lighting fixtures which produced a number of lamps that became classics. In 1974 Flos took over Arteluce. Flos lamps include the Relemme pendant lamp, the Tolo floor lamp and the Taccia table lamp, designed by Achille and Pier Giacomo Castiglioni.

Later lamps included the Viscontea, Taraxacum and Gatto, also designed by the Castiglioni brothers, and Fantasma by Tobia Scarpa.

Fog & Mørup (Danish): from 1906 the company specialised in lighting and opened its first factory in 1915. In 1957 Johannes Hammerborg became head of design and his sleek and innovative modernist designs became the trademark style of the company throughout the 1960s and 70s.

Herbert Terry (British): established in 1857 by Herbert Terry. In 1934 George Cawardine, an automotive engineer designed the Anglepoise with a heavy base for stability and a shade which could concentrate the beam on specific points without causing dazzle. It was introduced in 1936 and remained in production with refined versions for thirty years.

This early example of the Anglepoise lamp made by Herbert Terry in the 1930s has been cleaned, polished up and rewired and is ready to start a new life. (Photo: Morris Interiors)

Le Klint: Tage Klint founded his business in 1943 to sell the family's folded lampshades. He added a 'collar' to fix the shade to a metal stand.

Louis Poulsen: in the 1920s this company turned from marketing tools and electrical supplies to concentrate on lighting, notably the designs of Poul Henningsen. Henningsen called himself an architect and lighting engineer. He put a lot of technical research into finding a way of using electric light that would bring back the warm glow of candles and that would not be too bright and glaring. He worked from 1920–24 to 'tame the electric light bulb'. The PH lamp he designed is today a classic design and is still being manufactured by Poulsen. The company has worked with many well-known designers including Arne Jacobsen and Verner Panton.

Lyfa: during the 1930s the Danish lighting company produced a range of table lamps with similarities to Poul Henningsen's PH lamp. The company comissioned many prominent architects and designers including Piet Hein, Finn Juhl and Claus Bonderup to produce high-quality, original lighting which took advantage of new technologies and materials. Throughout the 50s, 60s and 70s, Lyfa's designs won numerous awards. Some lights juxtaposed parallel metal plates at precise distances with surfaces painted to create specific colour effects such as the impression of a spectrum, changing as the amount of ambient light increased or decreased, emphasising the lamp's role as an artwork as well as a functional device. In the mid 1970s Lyfa merged with Fog & Mørup but the brands were always kept completely separate. At the beginning of the 1980s Lyfa-Fog & Mørup was taken over by a mass-market lighting producer, Lyskaer.

O-Luce (Italian): founded by Giuseppe Ostuni in 1945. Worked with many designers including the Castiglioni brothers, Jo Columbo, and Tito Agnolli who designed the ultra-elegant floor lamp '363' with its delicate feet and slim stem in 1955.

Stilnovo (Italian): founded in 1950 and active in the 1950s and 60s with a wide range of wall and floor lamps, mostly by Italian designers such as Danilo and Corrado Aroldi and Joe Colombo.

CHAPTER FIVE

Practical Tips

It's not always easy to incorporate antique lamps into a modern home, except as decorative sculptures. However, there's no reason why lamps of any age or period shouldn't settle in well in any traditional or modern home, although it does help to think things through and choose lamps that will complement and enhance the decoration rather than have to be squeezed uncomfortably into a completely alien setting. Many antique and vintage lamps are fragile, however, and will need repair and restoration. This chapter has some ideas on how to care for your old lamps so that you will get most use or pleasure from them.

Modern attitudes to domestic lighting

Modern lighting technology has evolved particular ways of using artificial light to best advantage both aesthetically and practically, with a whole new language to describe the way light is projected and with different solutions for different tasks and situations. Words like 'uplighter' and 'downlighter', 'task lighting', 'general lighting' and 'accent lighting' are used as a matter of course these days when considering the most suitable lighting for any given room and often refer to the most sophisticated of modern lighting technologies and products.

But, of course, they can be applied to antique and vintage lights just as well. You first need to understand these terms and then you can apply them to your wonderful old lamps in your own traditional or modern home. Few people restoring a period house will want to return completely to the old labour-intensive and comparatively dim lighting of lamps fuelled by oil. But modern technology allows us to use a sophisticated range of light bulbs to create different sorts of light, low-voltage lights and recessed lights, but many similar effects can be achieved with old lamps and many can be restored or rewired to take smaller, more efficient bulbs than would have been possible when they were first used.

Dimmer switches are invaluable when using old fixtures, enabling a modern degree of illumination or a more natural, gentler light. Candle bulbs are supplied as 25, 40 or 60 watts and any of these are suitable to use with most fixtures.

The atmosphere of a room depends greatly on lighting. Period interiors can be enhanced through the clever use of modern electric fittings and modern interiors can often be equally enhanced by the sensitive use of old ones. The gloom of candlelight is congenial for entertaining purposes as can be seen by the wide use of tea lights in tiny holders today. Antique chandeliers, candelabra and wall sconces that have not been converted to electricity can create a charming interior environment. They look fantastic especially when furnished with good quality candles, even if they are rarely used. Candlesticks on the dining table have never gone out of use; their position and height is important so they do not dazzle people trying to communicate with each other across the table. But, of course, even if you don't actually light them, paraffin/kerosene and gas lights are nearly always beautiful objects in their own right and can rightfully be given a place of honour in the home.

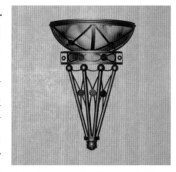

An attractive Art Deco uplighter glowing on the wall; this one is there as much for decoration as for serious general lighting.

Vintage bulbs

Most paraffin/kerosene/gas lamps can be, or have already been, converted to electricity. Gas lamps are obvious candidates since their hollow pipes are ideal for carrying the electric lead. One of the important things to remember is not to use too bright a light bulb in the lamp. All these lamps were made for the slightly flickering, slightly yellow light produced by liquid fuels and they really look their best given that sort of light.

To get the best from a lamp from the past, you might like to use antique-style light bulbs which can help recreate their original effect. Some of these are made in the original factories using the same machinery as the originals, so you can really feel they are contributing to an authentic look. It is possible to find light bulbs to complement a Victorian chandelier or an early lamp. Many Art Nouveau lamps have glass globes or shades that really benefit from a bulb that emulates the old fuel-powered lamps and will cast a warm glow round the room, making the best of the lamp's decorative patterns and colours.

This Tiffany-style art glass lamp is a downlighter, designed to cast its light down towards the table and items on it.

A paraffin/kerosene wick lamp can produce the shadowy, mysterious lighting that used to be the norm in every household. Even an unlit one can effectively hint at the past.

Some traditional lighting techniques

- Bedroom lighting often consisted of just one candle carried up to the room at bedtime.
- Picture lighting was provided by a couple of candlestands set down directly in front of the picture.
- A writing desk would be lit from above by one- or two-branched candelabra standing on top of a bureau.
- General room lighting could be provided by Argand wall sconces with white glass shades.
- There might be a hanging chandelier in the centre of the room if it was a room for entertaining or in a very wealthy home. This would be supported by several wall sconces, often using mirrors to enhance and reflect the light.
- During the nineteenth century small glass saucers were made with glass shades to cover a 'night-light' candle. These could safely be left burning in a child's bedroom until the child was asleep and the candle or night-light would then burn itself out.
- Kitchen lighting could be provided by wall sconces and/or pendants, perhaps with candelabra on the sideboard.
- In the dining room the main light would be provided by a pendant lamp over the table. This could be raised or lowered to make it either more general or more intimate and would be augmented by wall sconces and candelabra.
- Oil lamps with mantles provided enough light for a group of people to gossip or play games together.
- Student lamps and lamps with reflectors and/or shades were used to read and study by.
- Around 1915 the cloth-covered stranded electric wire was introduced, allowing exposed wires to be strung through a chain, and many chain-hung lighting fixtures were introduced.

A rise-and-fall mechanism can allow a pendant lamp to be raised or lowered according to the situation, and also for cleaning.

Vintage lighting round the house

This is a glance round the areas in a home that need to be lit and the sort of antique or vintage lighting that would be suitable. I have suggested some possible styles of lamps for different styles and periods. These are for easy and quick reference and are certainly not *de rigueur* unless you want to light your home strictly according to a particular period. The eyes are capable of adapting to a wide range of brightness but what they do not like is too great a contrast. So don't leave the working part of the kitchen in complete darkness when sitting at the table but reduce the light elsewhere in the room so that it seems to recede. Do think of introducing dimmer switches for rooms that have a dual purpose. That way you can be flexible about where in a room you want the most light without extinguishing other lights completely.

Milk glass globes were a great favourite with Art Deco designers and can still give a pleasant glow while producing efficient illumination, especially in hallways and corridors.

Halls, staircases and passageways

The entrance to your home should be warm and welcoming. In a small or cramped lobby it is not always easy to achieve this, especially if the space is box-like.

- Victorian swan-neck gas lamps with pretty little frilly glass shades can be the answer, especially in a traditional home and especially used with the sort of small floral-pattern wallpaper the Victorians liked. Such lights can face up or down and are unashamedly decorative. They don't take up too much space and if the swan-neck seems to stick out too far, candle-holders designed to fix tight against the wall take up less space.
- Eighteenth-century hall lamps consisted of a candle enclosed in a glass case so it wouldn't blow out when the door was opened. Such lamps, now converted to electricity, can be fitted with candle bulbs. Available in various metals and various shapes and sizes.
- For more modern small lobbies in apartment blocks or converted houses Art Deco sconces are ideal. They cling to the wall, are undeniably attractive and give an efficient glow without glaring.
- Large, generous hallways can be complemented by chandeliers, perhaps of the Arts and Crafts kind rather than fountains of crystal, although if you are the lucky owner of a grand hallway, particularly if it has marble and columns, a grand French chandelier might be appropriate.
- In corridors and particularly in narrow ones a series of similar lamps along the length of the passage will give continuity and more efficient lighting than just one point of light. A wall light or sconce that does

A covered terrace can be adequately lit with hanging lanterns. All too often such areas are over-lit, dimming the stars and removing all mystery from an al fresco evening.

not stick out into the passage will give a diffused light without getting in the way, and many Art Deco lamps are perfect for this.

- Staircase lighting is important. Many lamps suitable for halls and corridors will also be good for stairs but there are certain extra precautions to take. Make sure any lighting installation does not cast shadows on the staircase treads. The edge of each tread and the depth of the whole step should be clearly seen. Often a diffusing pendant lamp or an opaline glass globe can be the answer. There are many vintage 'designer' lamps from the later twentieth century designed specifically to reduce shadows.

The table lamp in this Victorian-style room has an extremely intricate porcelain base which includes playing cherubs and has a suitably gorgeous silk shade to go with its antique furniture.

Living rooms

The living room, of all rooms, is the one where you can match the lighting to your interior decoration. Living rooms have to perform several different functions and incorporate a varying number of people. It is a room used for reading, watching television, writing, playing games, showing off artworks, giving parties and often doubles as a dining room as well. All these require different types of lighting and so living room lighting has to be carefully thought through. The important thing is to have a flexible lighting system which you can orchestrate depending on the atmosphere you want to create and the tasks you want to do. Install several types of lighting and simply use the ones you want when you want them.

There is an enormous choice of lamps that were once designed for paraffin/kerosene, sold in their original state or converted to electricity; there are gasoliers and early electroliers with frilly and etched glass shades. These give a charming light for a pretty English or Colonial 'country' look where modern metal or 30s geometric designs would look out of place. In terms of style, Art Nouveau, Arts and Crafts, and many wonderful glass lamps such as those of Tiffany, there are also ceramic table lamps made out of ancient vases from China, Japan, England, France and Italy with plain or pleated shades.

Many homes have a central light fitting that was installed when the house was built. Central pendant lamps are widely available, either antiques from the Victorian period or vintage and retro pendants from the mid twentieth century. It is useful to have a lamp like this so that you can switch on a satisfactory general light when you first enter the room and then add other lighting as you please. Your choice of pendant will partly depend on your choice of period style and partly on the proportions of the room. Once you have chosen some form of general lighting you are free to consider how to tackle the more subtle and individual requirements of your life and chosen period and décor. For entertaining, the most comfortable lighting is probably provided by individual lamps in various parts of the room, providing pools of light that are bright enough to see by but flattering to faces.

- Owners of historic houses often enjoy lighting them as nearly as possible in the style of the time when they were built. Many such home-owners still use traditional pricket candlesticks, wall candlesticks with silver reflector panels and floor-standing iron candlesticks with no overhead lights at all. It is still possible to get candle-holders that were made at the same time as the house, not just in the style thereof. Although comparatively few people have medieval or even very old houses, many do admire and enjoy the softness and warmth of such lighting and can use a similar sort of lighting to get the general effect.

This room with its antique beams and bright white paint is lit by candle wall sconces converted to electricity which nevertheless retain the atmosphere of times past.

- As candles were the main form of lighting during the eighteenth century, so candlesticks, candelabra and chandeliers are all good choices for Georgian or Colonial-style homes. Many have been converted to electricity with candle bulbs. You will find them in iron, brass, silver or silver plate. Candelabra can have two arms or many arms and will provide that much more light, but remember that except for the mansions of the extremely rich, the eighteenth-century interior was what we would consider very dimly lit indeed.
- Simple pendant bowls suit many types of periods of interior where their simplicity will not clash with the rest of the décor.
- Chandeliers can look wonderful. There are many types, some exceedingly sophisticated and glittering but choose one in keeping with your own décor and the dimensions of the room. A small chandelier, perhaps from the Arts and Crafts period with several arms and a small shade for each bulb will give a satisfactory light and look highly decorative in a room with a comparatively tall ceiling with hand-crafted furniture and print wallpaper and curtains. A crystal chandelier can go in a living room but hardly as everyday general lighting. Such a chandelier requires proportions and decorations to complement it, a tall ceiling, and length and width all in proportion, plenty of wall space, preferably with mirrors to reflect the glitter of the chandelier. Chandeliers like this are truly for special occasions.

- So many lamps originally designed for paraffin/ kerosene did provide pools of light, some of them in sculptural clean lines, others lavishly decorated with various kinds of etching, frosting or painting. These include unabashed 'pretty' Victorian lamps, like the parlour lamps (often called 'Gone with the Wind' lamps because they featured in the film) which were popular in America, Tiffany's wonderful nature-flaunting opalescent Art Nouveau lamps and similar lamps made by other talented American designers, austere Arts and Crafts lamps with demure wooden stems and simple, angular parchment or stained glass shades. Then there are the many table lamps from the Art Deco period, geometric or flowing, with feminine figures holding the light source.

- Ceramic lamp bases, purpose-made or converted from antique decorative vases, also make good 'pools of light', particularly suitable for the English country look with upholstered armchairs and Jacobean-style floral loose covers. The ceramic part is highlit by the light bulb and the shade can be chosen to match the décor of the room or to contrast with it. The shade diffuses light and disseminates it. The choice of colour will make a difference to the final effect. Dark shades will allow less light through than pale ones and the shade can be used to add a touch of colour during daytime. Shades can be pleated, patterned, parchment or fabric, deep and narrow or wide and shallow but they must always be large enough for the base.

- The living room is also a good place to display a collection of antique lamps that are not necessarily for use. TV lamps, for example, can be displayed on top of a TV or, if you have a flat screen, perhaps on a shelf behind or nearby. Shelves in a niche or a glass-fronted cabinet can display a collection of little fairy or night-lights from the Victorian period. Candlesticks, of course, are easy to incorporate into a modern home and can look charming.

- Look critically at the room before choosing any lamps. A stained glass sunburst shade will look odd

This small chandelier fits the cosy lounge area of a restaurant to perfection and is very much at home with the branched candelabra on the table.

Candlesticks, chandeliers and candelabra are all relevant forms of lighting for a traditional house. This small cottage is using a suitably modest candlestick on its lace-covered round table.

with a chintz and small print English rose look, but beautiful with the squared-off shapes of an Art Deco interior.

- For reading, standard lamps give a good light while being stately enough to complement the 'best' room. These can be uplighters, providing a diffuse light that also acts as a general light but provides enough illumination to see by if you are in a chair nearby.
- Wall sconces are popular as a contribution to the general lighting and to provide the cosy feeling of pools of light. They are available in many Victorian lamps and also Art Deco and high-tech modern. Shallow bowls, casting their light upwards were popular from the 1980s.
- There is a good choice of modern 'designer' lamps intended specifically to provide small areas of light in an interesting form. For example, many Scandinavian and Italian designs using modern materials with a spare, sculptural look.

Standard lamps were a popular way of lighting behind a chair or sofa. This one with its wooden barley sugar twist stand and silk shade is very elegant.

Kitchens

No matter how well-planned or streamlined, the kitchen is one of the most complex rooms in the house when it comes to lighting. In the first place it is a workshop for the cook. Often it doubles up as a breakfast bar and it may even be the dining room or the meeting-place for a whole family, so here you require general lighting, as always. But it's also important to be able to see into cupboards, both high and low, and to be able to see when working at the sink or food preparation area. You need especially good task lighting over worktops, where you may be using sharp implements.

You may also want to have some form of highlighting to show off a decorative dresser or special tea or dinner service. There was a period during the 1940s and 50s when the kitchen was considered rather like a hospital operating theatre with smooth, shiny, 'hygienic' surfaces, fitted cupboards covering every wall, and white appliances. While hygiene is undoubtedly important, there is a more relaxed feeling to kitchens nowadays and many people like the Victorian look with its individual pieces of furniture rather than a complete 'run' of one design. Walls

A traditional old-fashioned upholstered armchair is complemented by the old-fashioned paraffin/ kerosene lamp which has not been converted to electricity.

are sometimes covered in floral wallpaper and wooden furniture and units are often brightly painted and accompanied by stainless steel appliances. Vintage lights of many kinds can be used in many styles of kitchen as long as they conform to the above requirements.

This old English lamp is ripe for conversion to electricity. With a little brass polish it could soon look like new, and take its place on a kitchen dresser.

- For an eighteenth-century look try simple four-arm chandeliers as general lighting; candlesticks converted to electric candle bulbs; candle wall sconces with mirrors converted to electric candle bulbs.
- For a nineteenth-century look try swan-neck gasoliers or electroliers for general lighting; candle or gas wall sconces; converted paraffin/kerosene wall lamps, Art Nouveau and Arts and Crafts wall lamps.
- For a twentieth-century kitchen try a pendant electric glass globe or disc for general lighting; Art Deco wall sconces; internally silvered spotlamp fixtures; pendant downlighters over worktops.
- Over the sink and other work surfaces there should be a good bright light. If you are going for a traditional look, you might like to augment any antique lamps with subtle modern lighting that will light the worktops without clashing with other lights.
- If you are using uplighters, remember it is best to have a white ceiling that will reflect the light back down again – the darker the ceiling, the less effective the reflected light will be.
- Even if your kitchen is tiny, you will still need some background or general lighting. Because kitchens are so often clothed in cupboards, a pendant light can be good here. There are many simple bowl-shaped pendants which can look good and give a pleasant and efficient light. If the room is large with a table and more people congregating in it, a more sophisticated pendant can be good. For a traditional look an electrolier or a converted gasolier or even a pendant paraffin/kerosene lamp can be a charming way of lighting the room, particularly in a country-style kitchen boasting wooden tables, chairs and cupboards.
- If a small kitchen is also used as a breakfast bar or has a complete dining area and perhaps is used for homework or sorting out the bills, one of the most satisfactory forms of lighting is a simple pendant with a 'coolie' shade. And if it does really double up

This English paraffin lamp has been polished up and wired for electricity and now hangs in a country kitchen in North Yorkshire. (Photo: Country Oak Antiques)

as a dining room, a rise-and-fall lamp is ideal. For a rectangular table you may prefer to have two or more lights hanging down over it. Ex-factory lamps from the 1940s onwards can be the answer.

- In the kitchen it is doubly important that lamps are positioned so that they don't shine into your eyes or cast shadows over any work surface. It is best if lamps are placed directly above the worktop shining down, and for general lighting, a diffused light from an opalescent shade is better than a bright light which can glare.

These two lamps in white glass and brass, designed in the 1950s by the Italian designer Ignazio Gardelli, are a nice play on early paraffin/kerosene lamps. (Photo: Designs of Modernity)

Dining and eating areas

To own a separate dining room is something of a luxury in many town apartments. Most households have to cook and eat or live and eat in the same room – or perhaps all three. In this case flexibility is the answer. You will need the essential general lighting, to be switched off when eating, and light the dining table itself with lights low enough to be intimate yet illuminating enough so that people can see what they are eating. This can be provided by a diffusing pendant over the dining table – better still, a rise-and-fall pendant so that you can raise the light to give general lighting and lower it to give more intimate lighting for meals or any other use the table may have during the day.

Effects of light on colour

Where food is concerned colour is important for giving people an appetite or removing it! In the home a large proportion of light from fittings is reflected on two or more room surfaces before it finally alights on the table. At each contact with a coloured surface the light is changed by the reflection and absorption of colours, so that it finally ends up not necessarily the colour you expect. Sometimes the effect is charming, so that if you use a standard bulb with its yellowish colour in a room decorated in warm reds or yellow, through a pink shade onto an orange tablecloth, the result will be warm and pleasant. However, if you use the same bulb in a room mainly finished in dark greens and blues, the light may make meat, for example, appear a dirty brown colour and other foods equally unappetising.

A simple country house with wooden floors and free-standing furniture has a simple 'coolie hat' pendant with a rise-and-fall mechanism over the table.

- For an eighteenth-century look try a large or small crystal chandelier with rise-and-fall mechanism over the dining table; wall candelabra with mirrored sconces and candelabra (perhaps wired for electricity) on a sideboard and perhaps a floor-standing *torchère*.
- For a nineteenth-century look there is a choice of many styles and sizes of chandelier including one with a swan-neck metal frame with several arms on a rise-and-fall mechanism; consider using candelabra with prisms, either wall-mounted or standing on a sideboard.
- For a twentieth-century look there is a wide range of pendants, from chandeliers to modernist designs of many kinds. Candles set in nineteenth-century candlesticks or candelabra can stand on the table or on a sideboard to provide a little extra background lighting.

Perhaps a bit garish to be a true Tiffany product, this art glass lamp is boisterous and fun. It would brighten up a dining room dresser or the corner of a living room.

Work areas

- A work area is anywhere that light is needed for meticulous eye or eye-and-hand work, so it includes not just the 'garage workshop' but desks, homework tables, sewing corners, reading corners and computer rooms. Desk lamps should stand so that the lower edge of the shade is at about eye level with the person sitting at the desk.
- Working light has always been an essential and there were many oil lamps designed specifically for desks, many of which may be suitable for desk work today.
- A favourite desk lamp in the early twentieth century was a brass-legged, green or blue shaded 'banker's' lamp. For a twentieth-century look these rectangular green-shaded lamps can still be found or you can look for an Anglepoise or other angled lamp, or a low-voltage reading lamp of Italian, Scandinavian, English, German or US design.

Bedrooms

General lighting for bedrooms can be gentler and at a lower level than many other rooms and the colour of the shades more romantic, using reds and pinks, for example. Many modern bedrooms often have no general

This little metal bendy lamp was a common design of early electric desk lamps and for good reasons: it takes up little space and the bendy stem makes it flexible, while the shade directs the light efficiently.

lighting, that is to say there is no overhead light in the middle of the ceiling and reliance is placed on wall lights, bedside lights and table lamps on the desk or dressing table.

- In older homes, ceiling pendants are still popular and the antique and vintage market offers some wonderful choices, particularly of opaline glass globes, which diffuse the light pleasantly. There are also plenty of wall fittings to create pools of light which are much more restful than top lighting. You can use the dressing table to create little areas of light and the bedroom can be a good place to show off a TV light or a little collection of night or tea lights.

During the 1960s and 70s large and small stylised flowers and leaves decorated many items in the home and this collection of lampshades is typical, suitable for bedroom or living room.

- Whatever style you have chosen for your bedroom, the first priority has to be bedside reading lamps that can be switched on from the bed and by which you can read in comfort – and for a double bed, where an insomniac can read and a slumberer can continue to sleep. (Even when putting someone up on a bed-settee in the living room, this ability to turn on a reading light from the bed is essential.)
- If you luxuriate in a four-poster bed with a canopy you will need to have lights inside the canopy, either on a bedside table or wired into one of the uprights.
- For an eighteenth-century look try a simple two- or four-armed central chandelier or small crystal chandelier; candlesticks or candelabra converted to electricity.
- For a nineteenth-century look there is a large choice of candlesticks, gas wall lamps, gasoliers, electroliers, with paraffin/kerosene bedside lamps, perhaps with porcelain bases. Such lamps have usually been converted to electricity.
- For a twentieth-century look ceiling lamps can be chandeliers or twentieth-century modern of which there are many in different materials and designs; Art Deco reading lamps for the bedside are available in many designs. Italian designers and manufacturers produced many low-voltage reading lamps, with a transformer in the base, which can give adequate reading light without disturbing a partner.
- Antique Victorian lamps can complement a bedroom excellently. Their individuality, their enormously varied shapes and the charm of their designs mean that they can fit in perfectly with the personal feeling of a bedroom.
- Frilly fabric or glass shades go with frilly pillow cases, flounces, valances and drapes.
- Choose a bedside lamp which will not easily tip over. The light beam should shine onto the reading matter and not into the eyes, so the type of lamp and its position are both important.

- Ceramic vases or bowls make simple and effective bedside lamps and there are some wonderful lamps made out of antique Chinese, Japanese, English or European ceramic vases.

Bathrooms

Electricity and water make a dangerous combination, so if you want to use antique or vintage lights in the bathroom, make sure the bulbs are securely enclosed in glass or plastic shades and that they conform to lighting regulations. Most uplighters and wall sconces in general are not suitable for bathroom use. In Britain the light switch has to be placed outside the bathroom altogether or can only be operated by a pull-cord switch.

A converted two-branch candlestick converted to electricity makes a useful bedside light. If using tall, narrow candlesticks for the bedroom, make sure they are sturdy and can't be easily knocked over.

Large converted spaces such as factories/lofts/barns

Of course, here there is wonderful scope for using up really enormous chandeliers or lamps that were intended originally for some entirely different purpose. If the ceilings are high, then there are many chandeliers, ancient or vintage that will grace a large space. Floor lamps too can be tall, heavy, of a size that would seem overbearing in the normal living room. There are interesting lights for a large expanse of wall and in these sorts of rooms lamps from the second half of the twentieth century can be the perfect foil for modern, colourful or sculptural furniture and clean sculptured lines.

Useful information for collectors

Antique oil lamps

Most historic brass lamps can look decorative and interesting in modern homes, whether they are used for lighting or not. Collecting and displaying antique lamps is a great way to discover a part of history and a great way of adding interest to your home. Nineteenth-century oil lamps in best condition are liable to be expensive, but there are lamps to be bought in various conditions and they are not too difficult to clean up, particularly if you don't intend to actually use them. However, antique oil lamps today have often been converted to electricity, particularly as table lamps.

Most people don't want to use oil lamps as everyday lighting indoors but you could consider them as a charming way of providing a gentle light out of doors for parties or family evenings. You can find them at internet auctions, local sales and auctions, local antique stores and many websites across the internet.

Hints on looking for antique lamps

When setting out to buy an antique, it helps enormously if you know your subject. Even if you simply want a lamp that will grace your home in proportion and style, the more you know about genuine antiques, about reproductions and about periods and styles the better. There are many ways to find out more and the more you learn the more interested you will become.

- Catalogues are an excellent way of discovering about styles and also about manufacture. Original catalogues may be found from time to time but are now very expensive; however, many of the old catalogues have been reprinted and as reference material these can be invaluable.

This little old lamp lacks a chimney but could easily be cleaned up and put in working order. Chimneys of all sizes are still available through lamp restorers.

- Get to see and hold as many lamps as you can. It's all very well to buy from eBay but you won't really know what you're getting until it arrives on your doorstep and that's not the best way to learn the subject.
- Buy a lamp collectors' price guide.
- Read articles in magazines and online.
- Join a collectors' club.
- Visit antique shops.
- Attend antique fairs and shows.
- Visit museums.
- Ask questions – dealers are mostly knowledgeable and happy to share their knowledge.

Get to know your lamps

- Many of the china, earthenware and cut glass lamps of the nineteenth century that burned oil can be converted to electricity without harming the original. Glass oil lamps are not too difficult to find but pressed glass ones in certain patterns have considerable value and sell for top prices.
- Fairy and miniature lamps, coloured glass and cut glass lamps and lanterns made for various special purposes seem to appeal particularly to collectors.
- Coloured and art glass paraffin/kerosene lamps and those with fine decoration such as cutting, etching or overlay are usually more expensive than most pattern glass lamps.
- If an oil lamp takes your fancy, purely as a collector and not for use, make sure it is not a reproduction. Some reproductions have fake milk glass or alabaster bases.
- In America all street gas lights became collectors' items in 1957 when some from Baltimore (the first city to install gas fixtures along some of its streets in 1817) and

Reproduction lamps

Reproductions can be a snare for the unwary. There is a difference between reproductions and continuous runs of particular lamps. If a factory has continued in production of particular lamps since its inception, using the same tools, the same materials and the same techniques, it is not really a reproduction but a continuation of a design. Reproduction, however, means lamps made by other manufacturers as copies of well-known designs. One way to tell whether a vintage lamp is a reproduction or an original is to look at the framework. If this looks too clean and polished, the chances are it is a reproduction. Many reproduction lamps are made in the Far East and the metalwork frame can give away their *nouveau* origins.

Venetian chandeliers are often found to be reproductions rather than the original thing and there are hundreds of reproduction lamps sold side by side with antique lamps, particularly Victorian and twentieth-century, so always ask and always keep a sharp eye out, not just on the lamps themselves but for the labelling. You may find something described as say 'Tiffany-style' or 'in the style of Arts and Crafts'. This almost certainly means it is not actually Tiffany or Arts and Crafts. Some reproductions are fine but if you are seriously looking for something truly original or old, make sure you check.

Genuine old candlesticks and rushlight-holders from the seventeenth to the nineteenth centuries are few and far between nowadays, but reproductions are being produced in China and India that even experts find difficult to identify.

Telling old from new glass
There are certain things you can look for to distinguish old glass from new. Sometimes you can tell by the feel or look or thickness of the glass, the way it was moulded, and the colours. The more you look, hold and see, the better you will be able to distinguish one type from another.

Philadelphia (installed gas lights in 1835) were offered for public sale by a New York City department store. They were bought up quickly and ended up in driveways and entrances of homes in the suburbs.

Caring for antique lamps
An oil lamp is any vessel that holds oil, with an absorbent wick that sits in the oil and can be lit, producing heat or light. Once the development of kerosene/paraffin made mass-producing lamps profitable, oil lamps were made from metal, glass,

porcelain and other ceramics. What usually happened was that manufacturers produced the metal parts, i.e. the base and burner and bought the glass elsewhere. Many domestic oil lamps have a large glass globe on the bottom and a smaller glass chimney on top. Many of these globes are etched or painted in a variety of decorative designs and most of them were made by hand. In the main they are fragile and need delicate handling.

Here is another neglected but sturdy old paraffin/ kerosene lamp which would glow beautifully after some polishing up and a new wick and chimney.

Many antique and vintage lamps are likely to be a little fragile. The years will have affected their materials, some may be missing essential parts and old electric lamps will need re-wiring. Some lamps will already have been repaired, renovated and/or rewired by the dealer, but there are important things to look out for, especially if you intend to use the lamp and not just enjoy it as decoration.

In the old days every large house had its 'lamp room' in which one member of staff would spend all day just cleaning and maintaining the lamps; washing them, trimming the wicks, making them ready for the evening. Don't forget the light bulbs themselves while you are cleaning the fittings. Take the bulb out of its socket and wipe over with a damp cloth, but make sure it's dry before you put it back.

Maintenance of burners and wicks
Routine burner and wick maintenance is important if you intend to use your lamp. Efficient combustion will be hindered if the burner is dirty and if the wick is not properly maintained and trimmed. Kerosene or lamp oil deposits on the burner trap dust particles. The burner body, especially the perforations, must be cleaned periodically to prevent clogging and promote proper air flow. Wiping or dusting will generally accomplish the task but occasionally a good wash with a washing-up detergent will remove most of the accumulated dirt. Trimming evens up the surface and removes the charred portion of the wick. Flat wicks can be cut straight across with a sharp pair of scissors. You can also trim off the corners at a 45 degree angle, which produces a more controlled flame.

Care of old glass chimneys
Many old chimneys were hand-made and the tops often were hand-worked with crimping or petals of varying sizes. There are imperfections in the glass itself, straw marks, bubbles and so on, and these add charm and character. If you want to use your lamps it might be best to use reproduction chimneys as fine old chimneys are expensive and becoming more difficult to acquire. Also, many sizes of old lip or flange chimneys are difficult to get hold of.

A well cared-for art glass lamp can really enhance a traditional style or a modern interior. This pair looks jewel-like together with the dark wood and furniture.

These two workaday paraffin/ kerosene lamps are charming but would look even better with a wash and a polish. Old glass is fragile, so take great care when washing it.

Safety

- Paraffin/kerosene, petrol/gasoline and alcohol are all poisonous; if any of them get onto your skin wash them off with running water.
- Paraffin/kerosene, petrol/gasoline and alcohol all burn fiercely, so take great care when filling and lighting lamps.
- Old founts, old joints and valves often leak, so check they are in good order before adding fuel and trying to fire up a newly-acquired lamp.
- Old mantles containing thorium are radioactive – handle with care.
- Burn-off smoke contains beryllium which is deadly in small concentrations so burn off new mantles out of doors.
- Burning mantles consume oxygen, so only light up your lamps in well-ventilated places.
- Poor combustion produces carbon monoxide, a little of which can kill you – if it smokes, turn it off.
- Lantern tops and valves get hot – handle with care when in use.
- Always use the correct fuel – petrol/gasoline put into a lantern designed for paraffin/kerosene can have spectacular – and fatal – results.

Using an old oil lamp:

- When using old chimneys make sure the chimney is clean. Dirty chimneys can cause uneven heating which might make the chimney crack or break.
- Keep the wick clean and trimmed to produce an even flame. It will produce a better light and provide a more even heat distribution, especially to the sides of the chimney.
- When you first light the lamp, keep the flame low and allow the chimney to warm up gradually. After a few minutes the flame can be adjusted to the desired height. Remember that rapid changes in temperature may damage the glass.
- Make sure that oval-shaped chimneys are aligned properly in relation to the flame. The long axis of the chimney should be parallel to the wick.
- Check that the chimney is not too tightly fixed into the burner. This is especially important with Aladdin chimneys which twist and lock into the gallery and lip chimneys which are secured with a screw. Tighten the screw just enough to ensure the chimney is secure. As the chimney heats up it expands and needs a little space to do so.

Cleaning your antique lamp
Choosing and installing a coveted antique or vintage light is only the beginning of your relationship. To get the best from your lamp you must maintain and clean all fittings regularly, since light attracts moths and flies and the heat attracts dust. Regular cleaning means they won't get so dirty that it will be impossible to get them really clean. Regular cleaning will also ensure that a lamp operates efficiently and that the light is not prevented from getting through the grime.

- Vintage plastic lights can be grubby. Most plastic can be washed with diluted washing-up liquid, a phosphate-free cleaner and a melamine foam sponge (a Magic Eraser). Squirt a little of the detergent directly onto the shade and gently scrub with the sponge. You can do this under the shower or in the bath but make sure no electrical parts get wet.
- People who like to use paraffin/kerosene or gas lamps for, say, dining can usually buy them quite easily but they do create smoke which always leaves dirty deposits on walls and ceilings. Users of oil lamps used to protect their ceilings by fixing smoke-catchers or smoke bells above the burner, which were easy to remove and clean separately. If you do have such a lamp, maintenance is important, not just cleaning the exterior of the lamp but also keeping the working parts clean and the wick trimmed.
- Although electricity is cleaner than older fuels, fittings still become dirty, especially if cigarettes or cigars are smoked in the house. Tobacco smoke covers shades, fittings and reflectors in a remarkably short time. It is important, of course, that the fitting

should be allowed to dry before you replace it. Leave it in a warm place near a radiator or play a cool hairdryer over it. In kitchens, bathrooms and workrooms shades are more likely to get dusty and greasy than in other parts of the house. Wash shades and fittings more often in these areas, using a strong detergent if you think the fitting will stand up to it.

- Pendant fittings need regular attention; bowl lights can soon become filled with dead creatures. Always switch the electricity off, preferably at the mains. It is quickest and easiest in the long run to remove the fitting, but light fittings, once in place, are not always easy to remove, so you might do well to rub the whole thing over with a damp cloth while standing on a firm set of steps.

Once your lamp is cleaned up and in place, touch it as little as possible. A light dusting occasionally is the best thing. Shades made of separate pieces of glass should not be allowed to get too wet, which could weaken the joins.

Cleaning antique glass

Dust is the first thing you will encounter in an unrestored antique lamp. Wear gloves to protect your hands, as well as apron and glasses. Always handle antique glass very carefully and set it down on something soft such as a folded tea towel.

Glass shades should be washed a least twice a year. They can be cleaned with a commercially available product or a small amount of gentle washing-up liquid.

Chimneys of real oil lamps should be washed in mild detergent and warm water and cleaned with a chimney brush (like a little bottle-brush).

1. Dust gently to get as much removable dirt off as possible.
2. Remove anything sticky, including sticky labels with methylated spirits (mineral spirits) using a paper towel and just a little solvent. Rub the affected area gently until the stickiness has gone.
3. Glass can be washed in water. Use a plastic washing-up bowl rather than putting the glass directly into the sink. Fill the bowl with warm not hot water. Use a gentle cleaner such as a washing-up liquid.

Lamps like this glass one, prettily decorated with blue flowers, should only need dusting occasionally. If necessary run a damp cloth over it from time to time.

4. Use a very soft brush, a make-up brush for example, to clean the glass all over. Rather than use more powerful cleaners, repeat this process if you haven't removed all the dirt the first time. You may need various brushes if you need to get to hard-to-reach areas.
5. Fill the bowl with clean water and rinse the glass thoroughly.
6. Then dry with an old towel or clean dishcloth.

Cleaning lampshades

Shades have been made from a wide variety of materials including glass, parchment, plastics, wood shavings, paper, silk and more. Glass shades were made from many different types of glass, plain or decorated.

Antique beaded shades are much in demand today and fetch high prices. Original beading will almost certainly have to be rethreaded as the original thread becomes weak and brittle with age. You will need special beading needles and strong thread and it is a painstaking and time-consuming job, so if you are a busy person and not much into sewing, consider getting such lamps re-beaded by an expert.

- Antique or vintage lampshades can often be cleaned up satisfactorily. Make sure there are no holes in the shade and that the frame is in good condition. If there is extensive damage it would be best to take the shade to a professional restorer, who can find fabrics for restoration and fix the frame without adding to the damage. If there is no damage you may be able to remove the shade from the lamp. Remove the dust with a soft clean dry cloth, reaching every part of the shade and the frame.
- Fabric shades are not usually washable. Even washable fabrics may not have waterproof linings and if you do wash them, the metal frame may become rusty, so on the whole washing of fabric shades is not advisable. What you can do is dust them regularly and they can be rubbed over with a 'bread ball' (a piece of fresh non-crust bread, squeezed into a sort of eraser) or covered with fuller's earth and lightly brushed off. Silk lampshades should be cleaned professionally.

Original fabric shades, especially if made of some delicate material like silk, usually won't have survived but it is possible to have suitable shades made up or find them ready-made.

157

- Raffia, straw and basketwork shades should be vacuumed often and may be wiped with a damp cloth or rinsed out in detergent if you like, but make the solution weak and make sure you have rinsed it all off properly because any remaining detergent will be slightly sticky and attract more dust. Make sure to dry the whole thing quickly so the metal frame doesn't get rusty.
- Parchment should be wiped with a cloth wrung out in warm water with a little vinegar added. Leave it to dry before touching it because parchment becomes delicate when wet.

Protecting your chandelier

If you are going away for any length of time, you can protect a chandelier with a muslin bag.

To make a muslin bag:

1. Calculate the circumference of the chandelier by measuring the distance between the tips of two of the long arms and multiplying this figure by the number of long arms. Add an extra 460mm to allow for gathering, shrinkage and a French seam on one side. (In a French seam, one seam is made and then another over the first so that the raw edge of the fabric is enclosed within the seam, making a neat result that won't fray.)
2. Measure the height of the chandelier from the top of the glass parts to the lower finials in order to allow for the bulge; add to this figure the diameter of the chandelier, allowing extra for shrinkage and hems top and bottom for the drawstrings. The easiest way to measure the diameter is by taking the distance from the central stem to the top of a long arm and then doubling it.
3. Cut out a rectangle so that the length of the material, folded over, becomes the width of the bag. Close the side with a French seam.
4. Hem the top and bottom edges to form a casing through which to run the drawstrings. Take care not to leave any raw edges or loose threads which might catch on the glass pieces or wires.
5. Before covering the chandelier, wrap each light fitting and greasepan loosely in acid-free tissue paper to prevent the muslin from catching on the pins and wires.
6. With two people working from stepladders or a tower scaffold, slide the bag on from either side of the chandelier, drawing it up to the bottom of the chain, to which it should be attached by the drawstring. Then gather up the bottom of the bag with the other drawstring.

- Acrylic shades, often used for lighting in the late 1900s, should be wiped with warm soapy water. Use a small amount of anti-static polish to prevent dust being attracted back immediately. If the acrylic is scratched, use metal polish to conceal the scratches.
- Aluminium reflectors should be wiped with a clean, damp cloth or sponge. Make sure all detergent is rinsed off and buff up afterwards with a soft cloth or use metal polish.

Warning: touch any antique light shade as little and as seldom as possible. Delicate materials are best given a light dusting from time to time and nothing more. Burnishing a piece of satin glass will polish the satin finish away, leaving a glossy spot and greatly reducing the value as a collectible. Even friction from repeated ordinary handling, such as dusting with a cloth will eventually add glossy spots to the finish, so the most desirable pieces become rarer even when they are not broken or chipped.

Cleaning a chandelier

The characteristics that distinguish fine crystal are apparent to the naked eye. Possible imperfections include lack of clarity, bubbles, chips and scratches. What you want to see is an absence of flaws, perfect translucence, silky smooth surfaces and prismatic glints.

Some people clean their crystal chandeliers every few months because they enjoy handling the crystal and admiring it close up. Some clean every six or nine months and others advise that on the whole a chandelier should not need cleaning more than once a year. The reality is that crystal needs cleaning when it appears dusty or dull. To lengthen the time between thorough cleaning, dust lightly every two months or so with a feather duster, lint-free duster or make-up brush. In order to make cleaning a chandelier easier, it may be possible to install a rise-and-fall mechanism so that the chandelier can be lowered. A limiting device will hold it at a point some feet above the floor.

Warning: If you have any doubts about your ability to clean an expensive chandelier, get an expert to come and do it for you.

There are many spray-on chandelier cleaners on the market but they may contain ammonia

This impressive chandelier might pose a problem for cleaning and general care. If you only use it occasionally or if you are going away for a length of time, it might be worth making up a muslin bag as protection.

or other chemicals that will eventually degrade the chandelier's frame. You can use washing-up detergent or rubbing alcohol more safely. Make sure you stand on a sturdy pair of stepladders and not on any old convenient chair. Always turn the electricity off and give the bulbs time to cool down before you start work.

Technique 1:

1. If you are going to disassemble the chandelier of all the moveable parts, always make a diagram before you do so. Otherwise you will find it difficult or even impossible to put it together again. On the other hand it may not be necessary to take the crystals off to clean them.
2. Place a thick quilt on the floor under the chandelier to catch any prisms or other small pieces if they drop.
3. If cleaning the chandelier in situ, do not turn it to reach the different parts; keep it still and move around it. If you do need to turn it, it should be turned from left to right and not more than half a turn to prevent the centre stem from unscrewing. The centre stem that supports the chandelier is a metal tube or an iron gas pipe concealed by outer tubes of silvered brass or Sheffield plate. The glass stem pieces are separated by metal washers.
4. Remove trimmings and place pendants in a plastic colander. Use a small amount of a mild washing-up detergent and rinse the crystal drops well with hot water. Harsh household detergents are liable to blacken the metal pinnings and make them brittle.
5. When rinsing festoons under running water, hold them at full length with both hands to prevent them becoming tangled. Again, use a small amount of detergent and rinse well. You can lay out the separate small parts to dry on a folded tea towel or leave them in the colander to dry with a cloth later.
6. Clean the body of a crystal chandelier by simply dusting it with a dry lint-free cloth, then use a glass cleaner sprayed onto a cloth (not onto the fixture) and wipe and polish all the pieces. Paper kitchen towels and newspaper are excellent glass cleaners as well.
7. Clean the bulbs as above.
8. Brass fittings should simply be dusted; do not use metal or brass polish.

Technique 2
A simpler method for simpler chandeliers:

- Put a cleaning solution of one part isopropyl (rubbing) alcohol to three parts distilled water (or half and half methylated spirits and water) in a spray bottle.
- Wear white cotton gloves. Spray one glove with the solution and keep one glove dry. Stroke the crystal with the damp glove and wipe immediately with the dry glove.
- Rinse in distilled water and dry well.

Repairing a chandelier

Many chandeliers are found to have chipped lustres and broken candle nozzles, greasepans, branches and bowls.

Warning: As with cleaning, if you are unsure about repairing a valuable chandelier, call in a professional.

- Damaged load-bearing sections such as branches are sometimes repaired with metal collars, which are not normally noticed from ground level. They can be left if they are found to be sound.
- Smaller decorative parts, such as faceted spires and small crowns, may have been badly repaired with resin. It may be possible for a glass conservator to take these apart and rejoin them so that the repair is more secure and less evident. Where the damage is too severe it may be necessary to replace the piece with an exact glass replica or sometimes a matching second-hand piece can be supplied by a chandelier restorer.

Ideally these crystal droplets should be cleaned separately. If you want to dismantle the chandelier, always make a diagram before you do so or you may find it hard or impossible to put it together again.

- Lustres have tiny holes drilled in them which split if carelessly handled. If a lustre splits during handling, all pieces should be retained for reassembly by a glass conservator, as replacements are expensive. Splitting most often occurs when iron wire or ordinary pins have been used to thread the lustres together. Always use special brass pins and consult a chandelier restorer.
- Brass linking pins go between buttons, lustres and pans; some types of chandelier use silvered wire.
- Check for broken, weak or corroded linking pins or silvered wires and replace where necessary. Always use those specially manufactured for the purpose. Soft brass linking pins bend easily and yet have sufficient strength to support the lustres and pendants.
- The linking pins on long vertical chains of lustres should be strengthened by fusing the ends together so that they do not stretch and open, causing the chains to fail. This is a job for a specialist chandelier restorer.
- If the chandelier has been adapted for electricity, it is worthwhile changing all the light bulbs at the same time rather than have to constantly replace one or two which wastes time and risks damage.
- Always support the greasepan and nozzles by cupping one hand underneath to counterbalance the pressure required to insert the bulb.
- Glass candle tubes break easily if compressed and excessive pressure could even break the glass branch.

If you are going to incorporate genuinely antique chandeliers and wall sconces into a historic house, it is important they should be kept in good condition or you will let down your whole scheme.

Using an old oil lamp

You may buy an oil lamp that no longer has a burner. Original burners are scarce and if you can't afford an original you can buy a suitable burner, old or new, and attach it to the lamp's collar. Add a good lamp oil fluid (you can now get highly refined coloured and scented oils which create little smoke). Pour it into the reservoir before you put the burner on and allow it to soak up into the wick, and then use the small knob to adjust the wick. The higher you raise the wick, the higher the flame. Always use a chimney in proportion to the size of the lamp. There are a number of oil lamp types that are suitable for using out of doors, being strong, stable and weatherproof.

Carriage and other lamps

Carriage lamps were used when out in the carriage or pony trap at night. They were often made in the shape of hanging lanterns. They were mostly of brass, wrought iron or wood and were mounted on the carriage doors or side walls. The sturdy construction and design of the carriage lamp meant that many are still around and well suited to use as porch lights today. Other curious and interesting lamps include billiard lights, picture lights, and flush-mounted lamps for low ceilings.

Workmen's lanterns and lamps

There are dozens of different workmen's lanterns still to be found. They were used on the railways, the roads, on ships and in mines and factories. There were gimbel lights for ships and railway carriages. All these lamps had to put

This old workman's oil lamp could make an impressive garden light, less dazzling than many modern outdoor lamps.

up with a lot of hard wear and they were therefore extremely tough and weather- and wear-resistant. They often had bull's eye glass panels which were virtually unbreakable. The early lanterns used signal oil, whale oil, paraffin/kerosene and other types of fuel.

Railroad lanterns

Railway lanterns had metal 'cages' with a translucent globe to protect the light source. There were lanterns for different purposes; some were used as railway signals and some for inspecting trains at night; there were conductor and brakemen's lanterns; bridge lamps, turntable lanterns, reversing lanterns. Engineers and station masters had their own design of lantern to help in specific tasks.

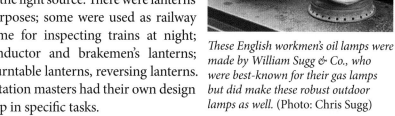

These English workmen's oil lamps were made by William Sugg & Co., who were best-known for their gas lamps but did make these robust outdoor lamps as well. (Photo: Chris Sugg)

In America train men's lanterns were used by railroad crew members and conductor lanterns were used on passenger trains; inspector's lanterns were used for inspecting trains in terminals and yards. Any lantern or globe with a railroad marking is especially valued by collectors. Many of these tough workhorse lamps were made by the pressure lamp manufacturers such as Tilley and Aladdin but among the first railroad lamps and lanterns in the USA were made by Archer Pancoast & Company, Dietz & Company, the Kelly Lamp Company, and Adams & Westlake (better known by its trademark Adlake). In all there were about forty companies producing large quantities of lights to the railroads. After World War Two storage batteries took over and oil-fuelled lamps were phased out.

Care of these lamps need only be minimal. They may be a bit battered but they won't have suffered fundamentally from the wear and tear of many years of hard work. The dents and scratches can be seen as the honourable scars of battle and long years of loyal service and should be displayed with pride. Many of them were painted bright colours, especially red or blue, others are a practical black. Use them as porch lamps, front gate lamps, garden or yard lamps and enjoy their rude health and solid reliability.

CHAPTER SIX

Information and Directory

GLOSSARY

Acid-engraving (etching): acid is used on glass or silver to give the effect of true engraving but with shallower lines.

Alabaster: a form of translucent, pearl-like gypsum, an attractive stone for lamps, either for the shade alone or for the whole lamp.

Alloy: a combination of two or more metals.

Ampere (amp): an internationally agreed unit of electric current.

Argand lamp: a lamp with a tubular wick invented by Aimé Argand in 1780. It increased the light produced to about six to ten candles.

Astral lamp: literally 'star-like'; a form of Argand lamp very similar to a Sinumbra lamp (*qv*).

Backplate: metal or wooden plate used to fix lights and sconces to the wall or ceiling. A metal backplate would help to reflect the light.

Bakelite: brand name for one of the first synthetic plastics made from phenolic resin.

Bayonet fitting: standard type of light bulb base with two 'ears' for attaching the bulb to a lamp socket. Used in the UK.

Bulb: the glass bubble that protects the light source. This is known as a 'lamp' in the trade.

Cameo glass: a luxury form of glass produced by etching and carving through fused layers of different coloured glass to produce designs with opaque glass figures and motifs on a dark background.

Candela: Basic international unit of luminous intensity.

Candelabrum: a branched candlestick.

Candle power (cp): a unit for measuring the quantity of light.

Candlestand: stand designed to hold a candlestick often made up of a column rising from tripod legs and supporting a circular tray. English candlestands were often made of oak or walnut, 3–5in (7–12cm) tall with scroll feet.

Candlewood: the resinous wood of any of several trees (such as bog pine) used for torches and candle substitutes.

Chamberstick: candle or other light used to see the way to a bedroom at night.

Chandelier: decorative suspended light source often using crystal drops.

Chandler: candle-maker.

Chimney: a cylindrical glass with a bulbous section, open at each end, used on oil lamps and some gas fittings to direct air and prevent draughts.

Chryselephantine: overlaid with gold and ivory.

Downlighter: a light fitting that casts light directly downwards.

Edison screw: the fitting on a lamp where the bulb is screwed into a socket. It was invented by Thomas Alva Edison and is more or less unchanged and available in two sizes.

Electrolier: a lighting fixture for holding a cluster of electric bulbs.

Enamel: opaque and coloured glass which is fused to the surface of other glass, ceramics or metals such as copper or brass to produce a raised design.

Facets: small, polished-plane surfaces on cut glass (usually crystal), often in diamond patterns.

Favrile glass: a wide range of brilliantly-coloured iridescent glass manufactured by Louis Comfort Tiffany from 1893.

Femme-fleur: a common theme for Art Nouveau table lamps which incorporated a woman in flowing clothing entwined with leaves and flowers.

Filament: a thin wire (nowadays usually of tungsten) which emits light when heated to incandescence.

Fin de siècle: describes the period at the end of the nineteenth century.

Finial: a terminating screw-on ornament usually made of brass or bronze which holds a lampshade in position. Finials are also used at the base of chandeliers, underneath candle cups and to hold ornaments in place on standard lamps.

Flambeau: lampshade made of opaque or tinted glass moulded in the shape of a flame.

Footcandle: unit for measuring light (USA).

Gasolier: a chandelier made specifically for gas lighting.

Girandole: a wall bracket from the pre-electric light era, usually incorporating a mirror.

Globe: decorative outer glass shade used on oil and gas lamps, although they were not always round in shape.

Holophane (also called 'stiletto' or 'prism'): a type of prismatic pressed glass popular for lampshades from the early 1900s because its refractive qualities maximised and evenly distributed the light without glare. The name, sometimes with a registered number, can be found impressed on the neck of the shade. There are three main types: 'intensive' for general illumination; 'extensive' for lateral illumination and 'focusing' for concentrated illumination to work by.

Incandescent: emitting light as a result of being heated to a white heat.

Iridescent: a glass or jewel which reflects light in interchanging colours similar to those produced by petrol on water.

Jugendstil: the name in Germany and Austria for Art Nouveau as it was promoted in the pages of the magazine *Jugend*. It tended to be more austere than French Art Nouveau.

Kayscrzinn: a pewter alloy with a bright silvery finish made by the German company J.P. Kayser & Sohn.

Lamp: in the trade this is the term for the tube or light bulb but for most people it indicates the light fitting and base and that is how the term is used in this book.

Lantern: a small rectangular lamp suspended usually to illuminate a hallway, vestibule or staircase, originally designed to protect a candle flame from draughts.

Lithophane: porcelain transparency which when viewed with normal reflected light has relatively nothing to be seen except that the porcelain is carved and is of various thicknesses but when there is a light behind the porcelain, the picture impressed into it comes to life and the full details are revealed vividly and in three dimensions. They were used among other things as lamp globes and half shades and as lantern shades.

Lustre: a drop-shaped piece of cut glass or crystal used as a decoration on a chandelier.

Lux: an internationally agreed unit used to measure the amount of light falling on a particular surface.

Mantle: the lacy, cylindrical tube fixed around a gas-jet to give incandescent light; the fabric or bead skirt attached to a circular or square metal or wood frame, suspended around a pendant gas or electric lamp to diffuse the light and prevent glare.

Mica: a translucent silicate found in granite which has a milky pearly lustre resembling glass and was used to make virtually unbreakable lampshades for gas lights.

Newel lamp: a newel is the post at the top or bottom of a flight of stairs; a newel lamp was fixed onto a newel post but the term is also used to describe any fixed table or desk lamp.

Pendant: light fitting suspended from the ceiling (normally gas or electric).

Pewter: an alloy composed mainly of tin with added lead (up to 80 per cent before 1907 but reduced to a maximum of 10 per cent after that date).

Pullman: a brass or copper table lamp on a short tripod base with one foot with a hole in it. Extensively manufactured from 1900 onwards and screwed onto tables in trains and ships.

Reflector shades: as their name implies these reflected and therefore doubled the light from a single source. They ranged from simple 'coolie' shades to pudding-basin shapes in iron with white enamelled interiors or green or amber glass with the inner part made of silvered glass. They were used especially for shop and sign displays and for desk and working lamps.

Rise-and-fall: a pendant light fitting counterbalanced with weights and pulleys so that it can be raised or lowered as required.

Rococo: describes an asymmetric decorative style incorporating scrolls, cartouches, shells and other curlicue patterns that started in Paris in the early eighteenth century. There was a revival of this style in the eighteenth century and in the Victorian era.

Sconce: a wall bracket with a backplate for reflecting light.

Secessionist: breakaway movement of young Viennese artists and craft workers from 1897 which led to the founding of the Vienna Workshops in 1903 by J. Hoffman and

K. Moser where they developed and manufactured items in a severely angular and geometric style. They were influenced by the British Arts and Crafts movement.

Shade: a cover for a bulb to prevent glare, control light distribution and/or diffuse and colour the light.

Silica: translucent material found in granite, far more durable than glass. Silica shades were labelled unbreakable.

Sinumbra lamp: literally 'without shade'; a form of Argand lamp in which the light source was at the centre of a circular fuel tank so that the light that fell on the table was shadowless.

Slip shade: individual glass shade sections that slip into place in a frame.

Smoke bell: a bell usually made of metal or glass which was suspended above pendant oil and gas lamps to help protect the ceilings and furnishings from the waste products of combustion.

Spelter: a form of impure zinc used for casting figurines which were often painted or bronzed.

Spermaceti: whale oil used for early lamps and candles.

Standard lamp: a tall lamp designed to stand on the floor.

Swan-neck: a gas wall bracket curved in the shape of a swan's neck with the lamp facing downwards.

Table lamp: a lamp designed to stand on a table, usually more decorative than a desk lamp.

Tallow: a mixture of animal fats, mostly from the suet of sheep and cattle, used in early lamps, candles and rushlights.

Tin: a silvery-white metal which resists corrosion and is used in alloys to make pewter and bronze.

Torchier (Torchière, Torchère): floor-standing lamp, casting the light upwards, originally with a bowl to carry a lamp or torch.

Uplighter: a wall- or floor-standing lamp which casts the light upwards so that it is reflected off the ceiling; popular between World War One and World War Two and again from the 1960s.

Vaseline glass: uranium glass is typically a pale yellowish-green and in the 1920s this led to its being nicknamed Vaseline glass as it was seen to resemble petroleum jelly, which was marketed as Vaseline at the time. Collectors still define Vaseline glass as transparent or semi-transparent uranium glass in this colour.

Vermeil: silver-gilt.

Volt: a unit expressing the potential of an electric circuit.

Wall bracket: a lighting unit designed to be attached to a wall.

Watt: a unit of power describing the electrical output of a bulb.

Wiener Werkstätte (United Workshops for Art in Craft): founded in Vienna in 1897 to gain greater recognition for arts and crafts. It became a successful commercial enterprise with its own workshops and showrooms.

BIBLIOGRAPHY

Bassi, Alberto, *Italian Lighting Design 1945–2000* (Electro Milano, 2004)

Dillon, Maureen, *Artificial Sunlight*: *a Social History of Domestic Lighting* (The National Trust, 2002)

Duncan, Alastair, *Art Nouveau and Art Deco Lighting* (Thames & Hudson, 1978)

Gordon, Mrs J.E.H., *Decorative Electricity, With a Chapter on Fire Risks by J.E.H. Gordon* (Low 1891 (reprinted General Books 2009 – Alice Mary Brandreth Butcher))

Marsden, Josie A., *Lamps and Lighting* (Guinness Publishing, 1990)

Meadows, Cecil A., *Discovering Oil Lamps* (Shire Publications, 2008)

Miller, Richard C. and John F. Solverson, *Student Lamps of the Victorian Era* (Antique Publications, 1992)

Paton, James, *Lamps, a Collector's Guide* (Souvenir Press, 1978)

Phillips, Barty, *Christopher Wray's Guide to Decorative Lighting* (Webb & Bower, 1987)

Potter, Norman and Douglas Jackson, *Tiffany* (Octopus, 1988)

Snape, Sarah (ed.), *Putting Back the Style: a Directory of Authentic Renovation* (Evans Bros. Ltd., 1982)

Thornton, Peter, *Authentic Décor: the Domestic Interior 1620–1920* (Weidenfeld & Nicolson, 1984)

Thuro, Catherine M.V., *Oil Lamps, the Kerosene Era in North America* (Collector Books and Thorncliffe House, 1994)

— , *Oil Lamps II, Glass Kerosene Lamps* (Collector Books and Thorncliffe House, 1994)

Wharton, Edith and Ogden Codman Jr., *The Decoration of Houses* (First published 1887, Classical America and Henry Hope Reed and W.W. Norton & Co. Inc., 1978)

DIRECTORY

Museums

UK

Biggar Gas Museum (this gasworks was still in operation in the mid-twentieth century. You can still get an excellent idea of the various processes required to produce gas.)
Gas Works Road
Biggar, near Peebles
Scotland
ML12 6DT
01899 221 050

Fakenham Museum of Gas and Local History (the only preserved complete gasworks in England. Good displays of gas appliances etc.)
Fakenham

Norfolk
NR21 7LA
01328 851 166
www.fakenhamgasmuseum.com

Murdoch House Museum (building reconstructed in the 1920s and home to Murdoch during his time in Cornwall and first in the world to be lit with coal gas in 1792. Small display linked to Murdoch.)
Cross Street
Redruth
Cornwall
TR15 2BU
01872 276474

Museum of Science and Industry (Gas Gallery)
Liverpool Road
Castlefield
Manchester
Lancashire
M3 4FP
0161 832 2244
www.mosi.org.uk

National Gas Museum (comprehensive collection, extensive displays on two floors.)
British Gas
Aylestone Road
Leicester
LE2 7QH
0116 250 3190
www.gasmuseum.co.uk

USA
Kelly Art Deco Light Museum (over 400 fixtures including hanging chandeliers, wall sconces and table lights.)
2000 Sims Way
Port Townsend
WA 98368
360 379 9030
www.thedecomuseum.com or www.vintagehardware.com/deco_museum

Information Sources

http://earlyelectrics.wordpress.com (a newsletter featuring industrial lighting. You will discover the unique character, rich variety and elegant simplicity of early utilitarian lights. These fixtures were born to be useful, brightening hospitals and dentists' surgeries, offices, laboratories, factories and other workplaces and date back to the beginnings of electric light. The wide range of shapes, sizes and designs on show offer all sorts of possibilities for your own interior décor.)

Clubs and Organisations

www.aladdincollectors.org (aim to kindle interest in Aladdin lamps and antique home lighting, provide educational information in displays and seminars, share information and provide a marketplace to buy and sell antique and collectible lamps.)

www.fairy-lamp.com (The Fairy Lamp Club was established in 1996 and is dedicated to the research and advancement of information on Victorian and contemporary candle-burning devices. It is the only club dedicated to this specialised collectible.)

www.historical-lighting.org (The Historical Lighting Society of Canada, a group of lighting enthusiasts from Canada, the US and around the world. Founded in 1981, they tend to focus on lighting of the kerosene era, although they have members who collect all types of lighting.)

www.internationalcolemancollectors.com (International Coleman Collectors Club [ICCC] provides information and assistance to Coleman collectors in the restoration and preservation of Coleman products.)

www.rushlight.org (The Rushlight Club was founded in 1932 for the study and preservation of lighting. Its aims are to stimulate interest in the study of early lighting including the use of early lighting devices and fuels, and the origins and development of each by means of written articles, lectures, exhibitions from private collectors etc.)

The Historic Lighting Club (for collectors of all kinds of antique lighting, specialising in English-made products but covering all European lighting (paraffin, petrol, manufactured gas, alcohol and other fuels).)
c/o Paul Mitchell (Membership Secretary)
PO Box 125
Wiswell
Clitheroe
Lancashire
BB7 9WH
England

Lamp traders/Showrooms/Restorers

UK

Alfie's Antique Market (dealers: row of terraced houses turned into an antique market with a hugely varied collection, upstairs and downstairs, of individual traders selling antique furniture and lots of lighting from Victorian to late twentieth-century, from modern to plastic pineapples.)
13–25 Church Street
Marylebone
London
NW8 8DT
020 7723 6066
www.alfiesantiques.com

Angell Antiques (interesting collection of largely twentieth-century antiques in which you may find some unusual lamps from all over Europe including, for example, enormous lanterns from the nineteenth and early twentieth century, Orrefors glass table lamps, 1930s film set lights or metal angled desk lamps.)
22 Church Street
London
NW8 8EP
020 7723 6575
www.angellantiques.com

Antique Chandeliers (trader: genuine antique chandeliers and antique lighting with an extensive choice of over fifty chandeliers available at any one time. These include large-scale English glass antique and crystal chandeliers, as well as a number of superb quality antique Flemish chandeliers and they often have examples of Baccarat, Osler and Perry. They also undertake antique lamp restoration.)
26 Sullivan Road
London
SW6 3DX
020 7371 7995
www.antiquechandeliers.co.uk

Antique Lighting Company (trader: stock of antique table lamps, wall lights, gas lights, stained glass lanterns and many other lantern types, sconces, lamp standards, gas lighting, chandeliers, Vaseline shades, Victorian and Edwardian fixtures, Arts and Crafts and Art Nouveau light fittings. Every restored light fitting is photographed and published on the website. Excellent online catalogue to order by phone or email. Visit the store by appointment only.)

Vintage Lighting

34 Dane Hill Road
Kennett
Newmarket
Suffolk
CB8 7QL
01638 751 354
www.antiquelights.co.uk

Antiques by Design; also trading as **Antique Sourcing Company** (dealers: create lamps from intriguing and memorable antique objects from riding boots to eighteenth-century flat irons and balustrades.)
Little Grange Farm
Woodham Mortimer
Nr Maldon
Essex
CM9 6TL
01245 222 771
www.antiquesbydesign.co.uk

Below Stairs of Hungerford (trader: antique shop specialising in items of the nineteenth and early twentieth century with five themed showrooms around a courtyard. Among a wealth of domestic antiques is a wide range of genuine original lighting and lampshades.)
103 High Street
Hungerford
Berkshire
RG17 ONB
01488 682 317
www.belowstairs.co.uk

Bleu (trader: antique, mid-century, modern vintage lighting and furniture; stock is classed as Twentieth Century Design, Modern Movement, Vintage Industrial Furniture and Storage, Retro Interior, Decorative Art.)
327 Railton Road
Herne Hill
London
SE23 0JN
020 7733 4999
www.bleufurniture.co.uk

Brownrigg @ Home Ltd. (trader: antique dealers with a good variety of lighting from antique wall sconces to table lamps with a selection of chandeliers. They always carry eighteenth- to mid twentieth-century lights among other interior and exterior antiques.)
Saddlers Row
Petworth
West Sussex
GU28 ODX
01798 344 321

Also at:
East House
East Street
West Sussex
GU28 OAB

Also at:
511 Kings Road
London
SW10 0TX
020 7352 7223
www.brownrigg-interiors.co.uk

Bygone Lighting (trader: wide range of antique lighting, all compatible with incandescent and low-energy light bulbs and rewired to modern specifications in Britain.)
The Brighton Lanes Antique Centre
12 Meeting House Lane
Brighton
BN1 1HB
01273 823 121
www.bygonelighting.co.uk

Caira Mandaglio (trader: French and Italian glass lighting from the 1930s to 1970s – also furniture, ceramics and sculpture from the same period.)
Arch 18
Kingsdown Close
Bartle Road
London
W10 6SW
020 7243 6035 (appointment only)
www.cairamandaglio.co.uk

Church Antiques (trader: enormous stock of pre-World War Two ecclesiastical furnishing – furniture and fixtures, including some serious candlesticks and other lighting from Britain's churches.)
Rivernook Farm
Sunnyside
Walton-on-Thames
Surrey
KT12 2ET
01932 252 736
www.churchantiques.com

Cohn & Co. (restorer: small family firm specialising in antique restoration chandeliers and candelabra. They have a large stock of antique spare parts and also a small number of chandeliers for sale.)
Unit 21
21 Wren Street
London
WC1X OHF
020 7278 3749
www.antique-chandeliers.co.uk

Country Oak Antiques (dealers: have been collecting antique oak and country furniture for twenty-five years. As well as candlesticks and rushlights, they sell oak dining tables, cupboards, coffers, longcase clocks, primitive Windsor chairs and period painted furniture and you can see the lighting in authentic room settings.)
Riverside Cellars
The Mill
Glasshouses
Harrogate
North Yorkshire
HG3 5QH
01423 711947
www.yorkshirecountrywines.co.uk/antiques

Crystal Corner (trader: Karen Matthews travels to Italy and across Europe to buy a wide range of antique chandeliers and wall lights. She will liaise with customers to find a chandelier right for the (taking in room size) ceiling height and decoration.)

9a Westhorpe Road
Marlow
Bucks
SL7 1LB
01628 488 868
www.crystal-corner.co.uk

Decoratum (trader: large 5,000 sq ft gallery specialising in original twentieth-century vintage designer lighting from the 1940s to the 1980s. Laid out as ten separate rooms with sixteen room settings, which allows clients to view the vintage lighting in a variety of interior surroundings.)
13–25 & 31–33 Church Street
Marylebone
London
NW8 8DT
020 7724 6969
www.decoratum.com

Delomosne & Son Ltd. (trader: established 1905, specialist dealers in English and Irish glass and European porcelain of the eighteenth and nineteenth centuries, including period chandeliers and other glass light fittings.)
Court Colose
North Wraxall
Chippenham
Wiltshire
SN14 7AD
01225 891 505
www.delomosne.co.uk

Designs of Modernity (trader: wide range of twentieth-century furniture and designer lighting, particularly from Denmark, America and Europe.)
Crystal Palace Antiques & Modern
Jasper Road
Crystal Palace
London
SE19 1SG
07966 285 694
www.designsofmodernity.com

English Lamp Company – formerly Stiffkey Lampshop (trader: specialises in antique English period lights and has a large collection of restored lamps from the Victorian, Edwardian, Art Nouveau, Arts and Crafts and Art Deco periods including gasoliers, lanterns, rise-and-fall, pendants, wall brackets, table and standard lamps. Also a lot of good reproduction.)
Church Farm Cottage
Barney
Fakenham
Norfolk
NR21 OAD
01328 878 586
www.englishlampcompany.co.uk

Exeter Antique Lighting Company (trader: wide range of lighting of various periods and categories including Art Deco, Art Nouveau and Arts & Crafts, ceiling lamps, crystal chandeliers, French *pate de verre*, lanterns, table lamps and wall lights. They will also source lights, restore, rewire and convert lamps.)
43 The Quay
Exeter
Devon
EX2 4AN
01392 433 604
www.antiquelightingcompany.com

Farriers Antiques (trader: a small but beautiful shop selling bespoke painted French-style furniture, vintage crystal chandeliers, stained glass table lamps and other antiques 'from shabby chic to vintage'.)
The Street
St Nicholas at Wade
Kent
CT7 ONR
01843 840 758

Fileman Antiques (trader: three-generation family firm specialising in eighteenth- and nineteenth-century English chandeliers, candelabra, wall lights, lustres and candlesticks. Have a restoration service including cleaning, rewiring, metalwork, glass repair and installation. Web catalogue has good information with the picture.)
Squirrels
Bayards
Horsham Road

Steyning
West Sussex
BN44 3AA
01903 813 229
www.filemanantiques.co.uk

Fiona McDonald (dealer: specialising in twentieth-century design with a good selection of wall lights, ceiling lights and lamps, as well as mirrors, seating and accessories.)
97 Munster Road
London
SW6 5RG
020 7731 3234
www.fionamcdonald.com

Frenchfinds Ltd. (trader: family business with a base in the Loire Valley region of France. Over fifteen years' experience selling French furniture, antiques and collectibles. Great variety of very elegant chandeliers.)
Strangman Street
Leek
Staffordshire
ST13 5DU
01538 370 052
www.frenchfinds.co.uk

Fritz Fryer Antique Lighting (trader: specialist in period lighting for over twenty-five years; superb showrooms; over 200 antique chandeliers, lanterns and table lamps. Standard lamps and wall sconces in a former malthouse. Also undertake restoration and make reproductions.)
23 Station Road
Ross-on-Wye
Herefordshire
HR9 7AG
01989 567 416
www.fritzfryer.co.uk

Harbour Antiques (trader: specialist in antique furniture and chandeliers from the eighteenth to the twentieth century including Georgian, Victorian and Edwardian.)
Hows Yard
New Road
Bideford

Vintage Lighting

North Devon
EX39 2BD
01237 425 545
www.harbourantiques.com

Hill House & Decorative Arts (trader: original antiques and lighting including Arts and Crafts, Gothic Revival, Aesthetic Movement, Art Nouveau, Modernism and European Antique pieces.)
40 Eaton Terrace
London
SW1W 8TS
020 7730 0629
www.hillhouse-antiques.co.uk

I Franks (trader: member dealer of the famous London Silver Vaults; sell enormously wide range of antique silver, sterling silver, Britannia silver, silver plate and Old Sheffield silver, including silver lighting through the Georgian and Victorian periods.)
9&11 London Silver Vaults
Chancery Lane
London
WC2A 1QS
020 7242 4035
www.ifranks.com

Kings Chandelier Services Ltd. (restorers: undertake repairs, renovation and restoration and cleaning for the trade and general public, using their extensive stock of genuine antique crystal, glass and brasswork at reasonable prices.)
202 Church Street
Witham
Essex
CM8 2JJ
01376 519 219
www.kingschandeliers.co.uk

Loran and Co. (trader: deals in Vintage Industrial, Arts and Crafts and Art Deco lighting – having found a lamp, they may sell it in its original form or turn it into something else, or you may find a bedpost turned into a standard lamp – go with an open mind and see what you may find.)
Unit 2
Manor Farm

Claverton
Bath
BA2 7BP
01225 447 277
www.loranandco.co.uk

Louise Verber (specialises in twentieth-century lighting in wide variety with many table lamps including Art Deco ceramic lamps, many floor-standing metal French foliage lamps, and a few unusual figurative lamps from the USA.)
Stand F070 and F080–84
Alfie's Antique Market
13–25 Church Street
London
NW8 8DT
020 7569 8770

Marchand Antiques (dealers: variety of antiques covering all the decorating styles and periods with stock from the sixteenth century through to the twentieth; including oak and walnut country furniture, antique French and Swedish painted furniture, Industrial Modernist, Art Deco, Art Nouveau, Arts and Crafts and mid-twentieth-century designer items including an interesting collection of lighting – some very unusual.)
40 Church Street
London
NW8 8EP
020 7724 9238
www.marchandantiques.co.uk

Miles Griffiths Antiques (trader: variety of nineteenth- and twentieth-century antique lamps including candlesticks, candelabra and lanterns.)
2/2a Shawbridge Street
Clitheroe
Lancashire
BB7 1LY
01200 443 658
www.milesgriffithsantiques.co.uk

Morris Interiors (trader: vintage metal industrial lighting and furniture that has been stripped, polished and sealed; stock from the 1930s to the 1950s.)

Vintage Lighting

641A Fulham Road
London
SW6 5PU
020 7610 6878
www.vintagesteelfurniture.co.uk

Paul's Emporium (dealer: antique furniture, retro, collectibles and lighting.)
386 York Way
London
N7 9LW
020 7607 3000

Philips and Sons in Lighting (trader: family business specialising in real chandeliers. They also have a huge number of crystals, wall lights and spares on their website and even more in their showrooms, all fully renovated.)
Unit 11
Riverside
Allens Business Park
Skellingthorpe
Saxilby
Lincoln
LN1 2LR
01522 704 400
www.philipsandsonsinlighting.co.uk

Retrouvius (dealers: specialise in architectural salvage and design; stock includes twentieth-century factory lamps and occasionally something extravagant (such as, recently, a pair of chandeliers salvaged from a Park Lane hotel).)
2A Ravensworth Road
Kensal Green
London
NW10 5NR
020 8960 6060
www.retrouvius.com

Sarah Scott Antiques and Chislehurst Antiques (traders: high-quality late Victorian or Edwardian antique gas light fittings and antique electric lights, known as gasoliers and electroliers respectively. Only sell genuine antiques: ceiling, wall, table and floor lamps, priced to include antique light shades unless otherwise indicated. All restored and rewired by professionals to modern standards. You will find examples of Arts and

Crafts, Art Nouveau and Victorian lighting.)
No 1 Castlegate Antiques Centre
1–3 Castlegate
Newark
Nottinghamshire
NG24 1AZ
07970 050 661/07773 345 266
www.antiquefurnishings.co.uk

Schmidmcdonagh (tiny shop with twentieth-century mostly German furniture, accessories and lots of lamps – some unusual treasures.)
24 Church Street
London
NW8 8EP
020 7724 7823/07802 498 066

W. Sitch & Co. (trader/restorer: family-run since 1776; five floors of lights, most from the early twentieth century; also manufacture a range of reproduction fittings following traditional methods; can convert vases into lamps.)
48 Berwick Street
London
W1F 8JD
020 7437 3776
www.wsitch.co.uk

Source Antiques (trader: specialises in twentieth-century antiques, architectural salvage and lighting. Lights include desk, wall, rise-and-fall, free-standing, pendant and outside lamps such as paraffin lanterns.)
Victoria Park Business Centre
Midland Road
Bath
BA1 3AX
01225 469 200
www.source-antiques.co.uk

Sugg Lighting Ltd. (trader/restorer: established 1837, reproduces antique lights using techniques and materials and some of the original tooling from early days; manufacture, reproduce and refurbish lighting projects worldwide.)
Foundry Lane
Horsham

Vintage Lighting

West Sussex
RH13 5PX
01293 540 111
www.sugglighting.co.uk

The Antique Chandelier (trader: antique and period chandeliers with an extremely diverse and very high-quality stock including nineteenth- and twentieth-century original chandeliers. Other services: metal refinishing, brass casting and refurbishment including supply of parts.)
47 West Street
Dorking
Surrey
RH4 1BU
01306 882 004
www.theantiquechandelier.co.uk

The Antique Shop (dealer: family-owned shop with Victorian and Edwardian furniture and plenty of Victorian glass oil lamps and lighting including chandeliers and ceramic table oil lamps.)
100 Bridge Road
Sutton Bridge
Spalding
Lincolnshire
PE12 9SA
01406 350 535
www.theantiqueshop.co.uk

The Old Cinema (dealer: sells antique, vintage and retro lighting and mirrors (also garden and hardware items and textiles).)
160 Chiswick High Road
London
W4 1PR
020 8995 4166
www.theoldcinema.co.uk

Tim Bowen Antiques (dealer: specialises in Welsh vernacular furniture and interior accessories.)
Ivy House
Ferryside
Carmarthenshire

SA17 5SS
01267 267 122
www.tim-bowen-antiques.com

Trainspotters Ltd. (trader: dealers in selective architectural salvage and period decorative items focusing on twentieth-century vintage lights and reclaimed industrial fittings. Specialise in sourcing good runs and quantities of items so are a good resource for large-scale commercial projects such as clubs, bars, shops, restaurants and pub spaces. All restored to a high standard and in 'ready-to-go' condition. Many come from Eastern European and ex-communist countries. There are many interesting factory lights, Holophanes, opaline globes, cinema lighting and some Art Deco – a recent history in themselves.)
Unit 1 The Warehouse
Libbys Drive
Stroud
Gloucestershire
GL5 1RN
01453 756 677
www.trainspotters.co.uk

Tudor Rose Antiques (trader: among wide range of antiques sells a good collection of genuine English antique lighting such as crystal and other chandeliers, lanterns, table lamps, floor lamps, ceiling lamps and gas lights.)
East Street
Petworth
West Sussex
GU28 OAB
01798 343 621
www.tudor-rose-antiques

Turn On (trader: shop jam-packed with a wide range of genuine antique lighting from many periods; most already restored and rewired including wall and table lamps and ceiling pendants. There are shades in etched glass, painted shades, articulated brass lamps designed for architects and vintage lamps from the twentieth century.)
11 Camden Passage
London
N1 8EA
020 7359 7616

Virginia Ashton Lamps (dealer: wide variety of lamps; period, decorated and antique, many in traditional styles and including table, standard and ceiling lamps, wall sconces and candlesticks. Others may be custom-made from unusual objects such as old croquet balls, tea caddies, etc.; all have been wired to UK standards. Clients' own vases, candlesticks etc. can be made into lamps.)
27 Newton Road
London
W2 5JR
020 7229 2577 (appointment only)
www.virginiaashtonlamps.com

Wax Antiques (specialise in silver with many Georgian silver candlesticks.)
49 Camden Passage
Islington
London
N1 8EA
020 7288 1939
www.waxantiques.com

Europe
Lumière de l'oeil (shop-studio and also museum of antique lighting with a magical collection of mainly European examples.)
4, Rue Flatters
75005 Paris
France
147 07 63 47
http://lumaria.perso.neuf.fr

Modernity (twentieth-century design in lighting with many iconic lights by well-known designers – also furniture, glass, textiles and more.)
Sibyllegatan 6
114 42 Stockholm
Sweden
8 20 80 25
www.modernity.se

Vintage Home (range of European and American designer furniture and lighting from the 1930s to the 1980s, shown 'in their natural environment in the way they would look at home'. Designers range from Borsani to Eames to Wegner, as well as a variety of mid-century Dutch designers.)

Daniel Stalpertstraat 97
1072 XD Amsterdam
Nederland
31206 790 472
www.vintagehome.nl

Canada
Romela Antique Lighting Inc. (trader: authentic antique European chandeliers, lamps and wall sconces; all restored and rewired ready for use.)
3216 Yonge Street
Toronto
Ontario
M4N-2L2
416 544 8251
www.romelaantiquelighting.com

Vancouver Architectural Antiques Ltd. (trader: Eric Cohen has a wonderful collection of antiques and lighting. He specialises in a diverse collection of nineteenth- and twentieth-century lighting from early Victorian through the Aesthetic, Arts and Crafts and Art Deco periods; all fully restored to viable use.)
2403 Main Street (at 8th)
Vancouver
British Columbia
VST 3E1
604 872 3131
www.vaaltd.ca

USA
Antique Lamp Co. and Gift Emporium (trader: hundreds of lighting fixtures, all guaranteed to be vintage from before 1940. All have been professionally restored to their specific period and newly-wired for modern convenience, and all glass is perfect unless otherwise noted.)
1213 Hertel Avenue
Buffalo
NY 14216
716 871 0508
www.antiquelampco.com

Antique Lamp Supply (replacement lamp parts: vast range of every conceivable part for every conceivable type of lamp including Aladdin lamps, with helpful instructions

for understanding replacement lamp part sizes, their proper installation and general kerosene lamp maintenance. Visit the huge showroom – take your old lamp with you – or order online.)
843 Old Morrison Hwy
McMinnville
Tennessee 37110
931 473 1906
www.antiquelampsupply.com

Antiquities (trader: gallery of museum quality. Antiques from around the world including Louis XVI and Art Deco pieces by Degue, Brandt, Galle and Tiffany.)
New York branch:
220 E 60th Street
New York
NY 10022
212 644 3403
Florida branch:
2736 E Oakland Park Blvd
Fort Lauderdale
FL 33306
954 565 4653 (appointment only)
www.antiquitiesweb.com

Appleton Antique Lighting (trader/restorer: original chandeliers, lamps and wall sconces in many styles including Moorish.)
801 Boylston Street
Rte 9
Chestnut Hill
MA 02467
617 566 5322
www.appletonlighting.com

Classic Lighting Emporium Inc. (trader/restorer: enormous selection of classic chandeliers, wall sconces, table lamps, floor lights, globes, shades, prisms and outdoor lights.)
1105 Frankford Avenue
Philadelphia
PA19125
215 625 9542
www.classic-lighting.com

C. Neri Antiques & Lighting (trader: large selection of American antique lights including crystal chandeliers, early electric chandeliers, jewelled pendants, sconces, newel post lights and table lamps.)
313 South Street
Philadelphia
PA 19147
215 923 6669
www.neriantiquelighting.com

Dalva Brothers (trader: wonderful collection of eighteenth-century French antiques including some very special candlesticks, sconces and candelabra.)
53 East 77th Street
New York
NY 10075
212 717 6600
www.dalvabrothers.com

French Accents Antiques (trader: an international company based in the USA, Italy and France. Diverse collection of European treasures including antique lighting.)
3600 Roland Avenue
Baltimore
Maryland 21211
410 467 8957 (appointment only)
www.faccents.com

Genuine Antique Lighting (trader: 3,000ft showroom/workshop displaying over 300 antique lights for ceilings and walls that date from 1850 to 1950; specialise in lights relevant to the local Boston architecture and will also work with customers who want to light modern rooms with renovated traditional lamps. Restoration workshop on site.)
59A Wareham Street
Boston
MA 02118
617 423 9790
www.genuineantiquelighting.net

Howard's Antique Lighting (trader/restorer: collects, restores and sells a wide variety of antique light fixtures dating from the 1890s to the 1940s, ranging from delicate gas-light fixtures to elegant chandeliers, which are all ready for installation.)

Rt. 23
203 Hillsdale Road
So. Egremont
MA
413 528 1232
www.howardsantiquelighting.com

J&M Antiques (trader/restorer: specialises in fine antique lighting of all kinds with a huge stock – also period furniture.)
6407 Transit Road
East Amherst
New York 14051
716 636 5874
www.eastamherstantiques.com

John & Rico's Antique Lighting (trader: gas lighting, chandeliers, table lamps, wall sconces, gas shades, solar lighting, Sinumbra lighting, girandole, interesting kerosene table lamps and more.)
Drawing Room of Newport
152–154 Spring Street
Newport
Rhode Island 02840
401 261 3980
www.drawrm.com

19th Century Lighting Co. (trader/restorer: deals in a huge range of restored high-quality and unusual Victorian patterned art glass lamps and lighting. Most lamps are offered in restored condition but in some cases are 'as found'. There is also a lamp and lighting restoration service and stock of replacement lamp parts for most antique lamps, as well as patterned art glass lamps.)
601 North Broadway Street
Union City
Michigan 49094
800 348 4552
www.19thcenturylighting.com

Objects in the Loft (trader: 6,000 sq ft gallery of Twentieth Century Modern design offering many interesting lamps including Eames era, vintage, retro, modernism, modernist, modern, twentieth-century, mid-century, Bauhaus.)

3611 S Dixie Hwy
West Palm Beach
FL 33405
561 659 0403
www.objectsintheloft.com

Paul Stamati (French Art Deco lamps by Edgar Brandt, Daum, Sabino, Lalique and others; also Art Deco furniture, rugs, sculptures and twentieth-century paintings.)
1050 2nd Avenue
New York
NY 10022
212 754 4533
www.stamati.com

Quality Lighting (restoration: of metal, spray-painting and colour-matching, updating electrical components, rewiring, pattern-making and mould-making. Visit by appointment only.)
Grass Valley
CA 95949
530 268 3795
www.qualitylighting.net

Rejuvenation (trader: in 1977 began as an architectural salvage store, then started making reproductions of Victorian and early twentieth-century ceiling fixtures and wall brackets based on specific antique lamps. Enormous range of excellent reproductions and wide range of genuine antique lamps as well. There are two retail stores or you can buy from the online catalogue.)
Portland store:
1100 SE Grand Avenue
Portland
OR 97214
503 238 1900
Seattle store:
2910 1st Avenue S (at Forest St)
Seattle
WA 98134
206 382 1901
www.rejuvenation.com

Richard Miller Lamps (trader: Richard and Cynthia Miller sell a wide range of antique, mostly Victorian lamps including student lamps, library lamps, parlour lamps, banquet and table lamps, stem and finger lamps, miniature lamps, leaded lamps, and reverse painted lamps, as well as gas lamps, early electric lighting fixtures, separate shades and accessories.)
309 East Main Street
Ravenna
Ohio 44266
330 296 6499
www.richardmillerlamps.com

Stuart F. Solomon Antiques (trader: range of antiques usually American in origin with a wide selection of Victorian lighting including Handel lamps, gas chandeliers, leaded lamps, table lamps, floor lamps and chandeliers.)
9–3/4 Market Street
Northampton
MA 01060
413 586 7776
www.ssolomon.com

The Lampworks (trader: purveyors of antique lighting and accessories; resource for collectors, restorers and dealers for lamp parts, ephemera and reference material.)
435 Main Street
Hurleyville
New York 12747
www.thelampworks.com

Websites

Dealers
www.allbelle.co.uk: UK-based dealer in vintage chandeliers, wall lights, mirrors, candelabra, crystal clear glass drops, ready-to-hang drops and chains, and fixing items.

www.antiquelampshop.com: Australian-based dealer selling wonderful Chinese, Japanese, English and French ceramic decorated vases converted into table lamps; good online information.

www.antiquelight.com: US-based online store, Allen's Antique Lighting, offers the finest in genuine antique lighting including antique gas lights, early antique electric and antique kerosene lights, antique chandeliers, gasoliers, transitional gas and electric light fixtures. Antique floor lights and lamps, table lights and lamps, wall sconces, wall brackets, etched and art glass light shades including Steuben, Tiffany, Quezal and other period artists. They also have exterior porch lights. No reproductions.

www.antiquesathillwoodfarms.com: US-based dealer offering fascinating furniture, accessories and lighting from seventeenth- and eighteenth-century American homes with an emphasis on form. Mostly in good condition but, happily, not over-restored. Helpful historical information and description with each piece. (Partnered with www.bluedogantiques.com)

www.antiqueslighting.com: US-based store; Joan Bogart sells antique lamps and chandeliers including Argand lamps, Astral lamps, Sinumbra lamps, kerosene and electric lamps, girandoles, sconces and candelabra.

www.artemission.com: UK-based online dealers; specialists in antiquities such as Greek, Roman and Byzantine including ancient oil lamps.

www.bluedogantiques.com: US-based dealer selling genuine early American antiques from the eighteenth century including furniture, textiles such as hooked rugs; specialises in early lighting including early tin sconces, betty lamps, standard lamps etc. Helpful historical information and description with each piece. (Partnered with www.antiquesathillwoodfarms.com)

www.cambridgeantiquelighting.co.uk: the large stock of fully restored antique lighting shown on this website ranges from Victorian gas lights which have been converted to electricity, to brass lamps and light fittings from the 1930s including Arts and Crafts and Art Nouveau; may include lamps from such manufacturers as Best & Lloyd, GEC, Edison & Swan, Tonks & Son – with many Holophane lampshades.

www.candlepower.nl: Holland-based store selling vintage candle-holders, divided into categories according to the material they have been made from and by time periods; they sell a wide variety of candles too.

www.chandelierparts.com: US-based online store for an enormous range of replacement chandelier parts including Swarovski prisms and Strass crystals, mostly imported from Europe, all cut and polished by hand.

www.classic-modern.co.uk: UK-based dealers in vintage modern lighting as well as textiles, rugs, ceramics and glass, plastics and metalware from the 1950s, 60s and 70s in design styles ranging from Scandinavian, mid-century modern through pop and op-art, space-age to psychedelic, some by well-known designers, others less well-known.

www.diomededecolamps.co.uk: good range of original Art Deco lamps, fully rewired to meet today's standards; good descriptions of each lamp.

www.davids-deco.com: US-based dealer in mainly Frankart lamps but also Ronson, Betty Beck and Nuart; also has information and articles on Frankart on the pages.

www.ferrowatt.com: US-based dealer with a range of antique-style light bulbs for use with antique lamps that will give a more genuine antique look than modern bulbs.

www.haes.co.uk: UK-based dealer in architectural antiques, salvage and lighting – lots of interesting pieces from local factories and schools.

www.honorstudentlamps.com: US-based dealers specialising in student lamps made approximately 100 years ago, which have been restored if necessary, cleaned and/or polished, sometimes electrified and described fully and accurately.

www.jonesantiquelighting.com: UK-based dealers, specialists in a wide variety of original antique lighting from 1860–1960.

www.leslieantiques.com: US-based dealer specialising in English Georgian glass and other antiques, American folk art; has some interesting lighting, e.g. a girandole depicting the last of the Mohicans, crusie lamps and English candlesticks.

www.moonlight-lighting.co.uk: restorers and dealers from 1800s to 1960s.

www.museum-of-pressurelamps.net: a great visual resource of an enormous number of pressure lamps collected by Uli Beck in Germany. There are eighteen manufacturers represented and dozens of models photographed. This is not an advice site, purely a visual museum.

www.peterwilletts.co.uk: dealers who buy, sell and restore genuine period lighting in a variety of styles, with particular emphasis on French items from the late nineteenth and early twentieth centuries including classic rise-and-fall fittings, chandeliers and converted gas lamps; all refurbished and re-wired to UK standards. Reproduction shades may have been fitted to replace those lost or damaged. Have a presence at antiques fairs throughout the year.

www.residentialrelics.com: US-based dealers who specialise in items that were built into homes from the late 1800s to the mid 1900s; no reproductions and no reproduction shades on antique lights; also lighting repairs and restoration services.

www.retrosixty.co.uk: UK-based dealers in mid twentieth-century design including wide selection of authentic original lamps, particularly Danish and American designs from the 1950s to the 1970s. Also authentic re-issues from the likes of Finn Juhl and Poul Kjaerholm.

www.salvagetree.co.uk: UK-based dealers in antique and vintage lighting from 1930s: opaline lighting to industrial factory lights, and distressed furniture.

www.sellingantiques.co.uk: search website for several antique dealers including lights and lighting.

www.shopcollectiblesonline.com: will lead you to an eBay site with a lighting category which has a wide variety of merchandise, from an Australian 'bear' night-light to carnival glass flutes to chandeliers.

www.theoillampstore.com: UK-based dealer and restorer of old oil lamps.

www.timbowenantiques: Wales-based antique dealer specialising in Welsh antiques including crusie lamps, candlesticks and weavers' loom lamps.

www.twentiethcenturyinteriors.com: dealers in 1950s, 60s and 70s furniture and lighting: 'We like to think we lean towards "modern" rather than "retro" in our selections.'

www.vintagelighting.com: US-based authentic original lighting from the age of gas lamps through Art Nouveau and Art Deco to twentieth-century, all rewired and restored to a high standard; old and new shades available.

www.vintagelights.com: US-based online store for wide range of genuine vintage lighting including wall, ceiling, porch, table lights and shades, including large selection of slip shades – also has catalogues, articles and newsletters so you can see what lighting would have been used in your home when it was built.

www.vintagelights.co.uk: UK-based online store of curious and interesting lights, particularly those from the 1920s, many from the US, Europe and the Middle East, refurbished and wired to UK specifications. Also choose unusual objects and turn them into lights.

www.vintagewonderlandchandeliers.com: dealer in chandeliers sourced from France, Belgium and Italy. Restored and revamped and fully rewired to conform to British standards, complete with ceiling bell and chain so they can be suspended or fixed flush to the ceiling.